ONLY AN EXCUSE?

ONLY AN EXCUSE?

DIARY OF A SEASON

Jonathan Watson & Philip Differ

BLACK & WHITE PUBLISHING

First published 2001
by Black & White Publishing Ltd

ISBN 1 902927 19 2

British Library Cataloguing in Publication Data:

A catalogue record for this book is available
from the British Library.

Cover design: Syntax

Typeset by Palimpsest Book Production Limited,
Polmont, Stirlingshire

Printed by Omnia Books Ltd, Bishopbriggs

ACKNOWLEDGEMENTS

The authors would like to express their gratitude to the backroom team who have been right behind them all season – Ann, Philip, Celine and Jack.

We would also like to thank David Stirling, Russell Kyle and Charles McGhee at the *Evening Times* for their support and BBC Scotland for their help in making this potential Nobel Literature Prize Winner possible.

JUNE 2000

THURSDAY, 1 JUNE 2000

The Bonetti brothers. Why did the Boss Marr pick them to lead
Dundee on to the next stage? Did he wake up one morning and
there was a horse's arse in his bed? Or had he seen a photo
of Ivano's lady and thought Dens Park could do with a little
glamour? One thing that does bother us, though. The Bonettis
are currently with an amateur side in the Italian Serie E (Fifth
Division) and they're moving to a Scottish Premier League club.
That's a hell of a step down.

SATURDAY, 3 JUNE

Have you seen *Rangers TV* yet? It's brilliant. A weekly message
from the chairman, a weekly insight into why the team are great
from manager Dick Advocaat, interviews with the top players
as well as features on all aspects of the club itself. Yes, you've
got to hand it to *Rangers TV* – or, as you probably know it,
Sportscene.

TUESDAY, 6 JUNE

Referees make mistakes the world over. Did you see the penalty
the ref gave in the French FA Cup Final? The Calais fans were
naturally distraught, gutted even, but not once did you hear
them sing: *'Qui est le Mason dans le noir?'*.

ONLY AN EXCUSE?

WEDNESDAY, 7 JUNE

This is a true story (and no, I haven't been drinking Bacardi Breezers). Many, many years ago when we were but spotty feather-cut lads of 17, we visited Montreux in Switzerland. While enjoying an extortionately priced Coca-Cola, the waiter asked me where I was from. 'Scotland,' I said, dead proud like. 'Ah,' smiled the waiter knowingly, 'Glasgow Ranjers'.

Point of the story? That Swiss waiters are mad enough to follow Scottish football? That *Scotsport* is one of the top comedy shows in Switzerland? That Celtic used to be the Scottish club everyone in Europe knew about and now it's Rangers? Of course, the Hoops have more to worry about than the mere fact that Rangers have overtaken them in the European fame stakes. The mood at Celtic Park is heavier than Matt McGlone's eyebrows. But we'd like to take this opportunity to clear up some of the things said about the club. Things like . . .

'The players are too scared to attend functions at supporters' clubs.' We can exclusively reveal that they have nothing to worry about. They'll get a great reception – as long as they stick to Rangers clubs.

'A clear-out is imminent and one of those who will be leaving is Jonathan Gould.' If this is true then we wouldn't mind a chat with him before he goes. We would love to ask him what is the scariest thing to face, a free kick from Jorg Albertz or a pass-back from Oliver Tebily?

'A new top-class, quality manager will be appointed within weeks, assuring us that the club are looking to the future.' When he makes his press conference entry, will he be accompanied by the Lisbon Lions?

THURSDAY, 8 JUNE

'Broadsword calling Danny Boy. Broadsword calling Danny Boy. Are you receiving me, over?' The theme from *Where Eagles Dare* blared out of our televisions, Kevin Keegan was portrayed in Churchillian manner and three former England bosses predicted victory for Blighty's finest. But when it came to the match itself England wobbled worse than the new Millennium Bridge. Right from the very start we could sense something was on here. First surprise came with the national anthems; David Beckham actually knew all the words of 'God Save the Queen'. Then came a selection shock; Kenny Rogers was in the Portugal line-up.

We were still debating whether Scholes' header had actually crossed the line or not when England went two up so we just thought that once again the English were going to have the luck of the Irish and get away with the points. But, thank goodness, in the end exceptional skill and technical ability overcame mediocrity and Portugal grabbed the victory. If any other team in the world were 2–0 up and lost 3–2 it would be a disaster. England do it and it's an 'epic'.

FRIDAY, 9 JUNE

Barry Davies' interesting fact of the week

Italy wear blue because it was the colour of the House of Savoy.

We have to admit neither of us had any idea that Italy used to frequent the long-closed, much lamented Savoy disco in Sauchiehall Street. Thanks, Barry, you learn something every day.

ONLY AN EXCUSE?

SATURDAY, 10 JUNE

Yes, yes, OK, we know, we know, but honestly, it's sheer coincidence that Italy wear blue and Hugh Dallas just so happened to give them a soft penalty. Hughie must have been feeling lonely out there after making such a controversial decision so it was nice of the Turkish fans to make him feel at home by pelting him with coins.

Funny thing about referees: we reckon it's how you look rather than what you do that earns you respect. Look at Señor Collina, Italy's answer to John Rowbotham. If you were a footballer, would you argue with someone who looks like Nosferatu the Vampire? Shug Dallas, on the other hand, just looks like a nice Boys Brigade leader, and whereas Collina's facial expression seems to be constantly saying, 'What are you looking at?' Shug's is more, 'What am I doing here?'. Anyway, no luck, Turkey. Not only did you get Hugh Dallas but – no offence – you've also got the worst national anthem we've heard so far.

SUNDAY, 11 JUNE

Ian Wright announcing this week that he was definitely retiring from football came as a surprise to us both. We thought he already had retired – halfway through his spell at Celtic Park.

MONDAY, 12 JUNE

You've got to hand it to *Lodge Sportscene*. Although off the air, they still manage to exert their influence over *Reporting Scotland*. The news that Inverness Caley Thistle and Ross County are getting together to start the Highland's first soccer academy seemed too good an excuse to miss the opportunity to once again show Caley's Scottish Cup goals against Celtic. Perhaps it's time *Sportscene* ran a competition on this one. How many times have the BBC shown Inverness Caley Thistle's goals against Celtic? Is it:

(a) 20 times?
(b) 100 times?
(c) not nearly enough times?

Answers on a postcard please, then throw the postcard in the bin.

You would have to say things are definitely looking up over at Celtic Park. Now there's a realistic confidence growing and it's all down to one man, Martin O'Neill. This guy hasn't so much kissed the Blarney Stone as taken a bite out of it. He's got the press eating out of his hand and has pulled the wool over their eyes to such an extent that no one's giving pelters for him not having signed at least six new players by now. And we're sure every Celtic supporter is desperate to find out if, in the next few weeks, Regi Blinker is to be offered a new contract or have a contract taken out on him, or if they will ever get a chance to see what Stephane Bonnes looks like before he's shipped back to France.

Honestly, though, we're glad to see something close to sanity returning to Parkhead because things were really starting to get daft. I mean, there was even talk of Mike Tyson coming to Celtic Park. But we ask you, is he any better than any of the players they have there already?

'DENIS LAW'

Well, you know, as I say, everyone's going on about these 2000 Euros, which they tell me is a lot of money but, to be honest, I don't want any Euros, I'm not sure at all about a European single currency, I don't know anything about electricity! So somebody said to me, 'OK then, Denis' – they call me Denis because that's my name – they said, 'OK then, Denis, do you prefer Pounds Sterling?' And I said, no, what use are pounds when you can only spend them at Sterling? What if you want to go to another furniture shop? See what I'm getting at?

Anyway, this competition to win the 2000 euros – Euro 2000 – I think it's a great idea playing it in the Low Countries because, being low, they are also very flat which means at least you are guaranteed a level playing field. But, of course, the big worry is all those soccer hooligans who'll be going over to cause trouble. But, you know, the government should look on the bright side. At least it's not the Women's Institute that is going.

Player of the tournament? I like David Edgars. He's cool, very cool, so cool in fact that he wears sunglasses when he's playing. Also look out for Tomas Rosicky of the Republic of Czech – you can't miss him, he looks like K.D. Lang, probably sings like her as well – Luis Figaro, the Portuguesian, their best player since the great Hugh Sabio – what a player Big Hughie was – and of course, Zinda ... Zanido ... Zidna ... that big French bloke, he's good as well.

Predictions as to who will win it? Well, usually I like to wait until after a competition has finished before I predict the outcome, but Holland look good, that's because they play in a style not unlike the Dutch. And you can never discount the Germans, they have so much self-belief, especially in themselves. But for me, OK, call me mad, call me crazy, call me controversial, call me completely ill-informed and existing on a totally different planet, but I'll go for a wild card, I'll go for Argentina.

FRIDAY, 16 JUNE

What about this new six-seconds rule for goalkeepers? I take it that will be introduced to Scotland next season. If they do and I was a Kilmarnock fan I'd be worried. When Gordon Marshall catches a ball it usually takes him at least six seconds to get over the shock.

SATURDAY, 17 JUNE

Catriona Bisset. Who's she? Only the first female woman to be made a chief executive at a Scottish Football Club. Catriona is a former Managing Director of the Littlejohn's restaurant chain so, if nothing else, the burgers will improve at Caley. You know, we have to say we're surprised this story didn't make the headlines on *Reporting Scotland*. Not like them to miss another great opportunity to air Caley's goals against Celtic in the Scottish Cup. After all, it's been nearly a week since they last showed them.

Clever old BBC, eh? No doubt smarting over losing *Match of the Day* and not having an afternoon match on Saturday, they played a masterstroke and showed *Babe*, a movie about a squeeky-voiced, whining piglet. They were obviously thinking a lot of footie fans would tune in and mistake it for Mark Lawrenson.

We don't want to say too much about the England/Germany match itself other than that has to be the worst German side we can remember ever! Tell you what the problem is? Too good looking. They've only got one world-class growler in the line-up, the truly hacket Jens Jeremies. The rest of them look like models from the pages of the *Empire* catalogue. What has happened to the nation who gave us such footballing 'dugs' as Günter Netzer, Gerd Müller and the awesome George Schwartzenbeck? I know they've got the pot-ugly Horst Hrubesch on the coaching staff, no doubt to give them ugly lessons, but it's just not working.

In terms of football, the once mighty Germany's lack of quality was summed up when they brought on substitute Michael Ballack. Who? Exactly. Ballack has four brothers, all professional footballers, all close to international standard, but coach Erich Ribbeck won't play them all in the same team. He refuses to have a team that plays like a load of Ballacks.

SUNDAY, 18 JUNE

What's the thing Rangers fans are always complaining about when they get dumped out of Europe – apart from the Germans being a bunch of cheating so-and-sos? How about that they don't get enough competition at domestic level so that when they come up against a real team in Europe the gulf in the standard of football cannot be bridged. So, really, it's not Rangers' fault when they get knocked out of Europe. It's all the other Scottish teams' fault for not being good enough to give Rangers a decent game every week. Fair point?

So why do Rangers do all they can to reduce the competition at domestic level by buying up all the other clubs' best players? And why all this talk about soccer academies and feeder clubs? Complete waste of time and money. We all know that in essence every club in Scotland – apart from Celtic – is a Rangers soccer academy and feeder club because whenever any club produces anybody who's any good – e.g. Kenny Miller of Hibs – the 'Gers will just flash the cheque book and make club and player an offer they can't refuse.

Celtic fans must be heartened by the roaring silence emanating from their club. How many players have Rangers signed now and how many more are still being linked with a move to Castle Greyskull? Why don't Celtic go for a name that would really capture the imagination? Why don't they sign Prince William? Did you see him play football in that 18th-birthday special? He was totally useless. However, just think how Rangers – a club with a vague-ish history of Royalist leanings – would feel if the future King of Great Britain and Ireland was playing in the Hoops? That would surely get their oldest rivals back for Mo Johnston with interest.

MONDAY, 19 JUNE

The Czech Republic, the first team to go out of Euro 2000. Was picking them as our 'dark horses' the kiss of death or what? Actually, the Czechs were pretty unlucky when you think about it. Hitting the woodwork twice against Holland and once against France at crucial times in the game. They kind of reminded us of Scotland. They even had a player whose name sums up what we always come away with in these tournaments: Fukal.

'GRAEME SOUNESS'

Can I just say something here? Yeah, for sure, I've always said that what Scotland boss, Craig Brown, needed to do was the same as what I did when I was boss of Rangers. Go out and sign a good, quality Englishman. Well, he didn't, he got Dominic Matteo instead. I have to say I never thought I'd see the day that Scotland would stoop so low that they'd be forced to play a man born in Dumfries!

I've been asked to give my opinion on a few matters. Now, to be fair, I don't know anything about some of the things I've been asked to comment on, but since when has that ever stopped me? First of all, should Beckham have given the fans the finger? I'd say, definitely no. He should not have made that gesture, he should have climbed over the fans and beat them to a pulp. In the past I might have suggested something more drastic. Obviously I have mellowed over the years.

Can I just say something else here? The latest batch of Honours to be handed out. Yeah, for sure, I think I was due something. For services to medicine, perhaps? Do you know that Scottish hospitals lead the world in the treatment of bruised shins and ankles thanks to all the practice they got when I played in Scotland? Or how about for services to entertainment? You don't think I was a bit of a comedian, look at some of the signings I made at Rangers. Surely signing Mel Sterland is worth a knighthood alone?

THURSDAY, 22 JUNE

So, former Celtic boss John Barnes has finally given an exclusive interview that reveals, for the first time, what went wrong in the dressing-room at half-time during the Caley game.

'For the first time?' We think not. A transcript of the half-time discussion has been available on just about every fan website in the country for months and it makes much more interesting reading than J.B.'s cleaned-up version. There are too many 'f's and 'c's for us to be able to repeat it but, interestingly enough, both Barnes' version and the version provided by the mate of a bloke whose uncle is married to the woman who changes the soap in the home dressing-room at Celtic Park are remarkably similar. So, it must be true then?

FRIDAY, 23 JUNE

Like everyone else we were happy to see England go out of Euro 2000, not because they are English but because they were rank rotten and they knew it. We were equally happy to see Germany and Norway go out for the exact same reasons, so no accusations of Anglophobia, please. It would have been a travesty had any of these teams reached the quarter-finals, although Norway's exit meant fans were denied the pleasure of playing 'what's he going to do next?' if Vidar Riseth got a game.

You do have to feel sorry for Kevin Keegan, though. The Scottish fitba' meedja gives Craig Brown pelters from time to time, but down South the main objective of the press seems to be to get the man they want made manager, then see how quickly they can get him the sack. On top of all this, you've now got one of Kevin's own players allegedly criticising the gaffer's tactics?

ONLY AN EXCUSE?

Martin Keown claims that what he said was misconstrued, though. He's supposed to have described England's tactics as 'inept'. Honestly, can you see Martin Keown using a big word like that?

SATURDAY, 24 JUNE

Rangers won the league by a mile last season and have already bought six players in the close season with the threat of a world-class – i.e. expensive, even if no one's ever heard of him – striker still to come. Celtic lost the League by a mile last season and have bought no one.

Are there any rocket scientists out there who could explain to us what that might mean? What is happening at Celtic? Have they any money at all, or are they saving it all up for a farewell pressie for Kenny Dalglish? I mean, there hasn't even been any word if Regi Blinker's contract is being renewed.

A couple of weeks back it was Belgium's Bart Goor who was at the top of the 'Tic list. But we had serious doubts about that one. 'Goor', you see, is pronounced 'Hoor', and you're slap bang in the middle of another 'Scheidt' scenario.

Of course, the big story is Chris Sutton. Chris Sutton, a name that has provoked a wave of unbridled apathy among most Celtic fans. He was up checking out Celtic Park and was well impressed; he has been up for games before; he sees himself as an adopted fan of the club – Celtic supporters can spot a jersey-kisser a mile off. If, however, the big nearly-England striker does say, 'OK, I'll take the 30 grand a week,' we have to say, we're wondering how the fans will react to former glamour – i.e. topless – model, Mrs Sutton. Maybe the club will make her feel more involved. Maybe *The Celtic View* will introduce a

Page Three Stunna? Maybe not, enough diddies on their pages as it is.

MONDAY, 26 JUNE

I know it's not really football-related, but it did happen at Hampden Park and the SFA made a few quid out of it so I suppose, in a vague sort of way, it is OK for us to say a few words about Tyson and Savarase. As George Bowie would say – and does, often – 'What was all that about?' At least Lou Savarase went 38 seconds. He must feel quite pleased that his fight with Tyson lasted a full 37 seconds longer than Frank Warren's.

As for the fight itself, well, to be honest, we thought Big Lou just might be a bit of a dud when we saw the gut hanging over the waistband of his boxers. To be honest, Tyson should have waited a fortnight and shared the Hampden bill with Tina Turner. We think she'd have given him more of a fight.

TUESDAY, 27 JUNE

So just imagine Scotland was successful with its bid to host Euro 2008, what then? Well . . . eh . . . can I phone a friend? Has anyone thought of the consequences of this folly? Has anyone considered the impact of all those foreigners coming over here, drinking all our bevvy and chatting up all our women? Has anyone thought of the humiliation of being the only host nation to go out the competition after one game? Has anyone thought that, realistically, we haven't a hope in hell of getting it?

Now, wait a second, are we putting Scotland down here? Are we denigrating dear old Caledonia? No. We're just being realistic.

First of all, in order to host such a competition, UEFA specify that the host nation must have between five and ten stadiums, each with a capacity of 30–50,000. How many have we got? Celtic Park, Ibrox Stadium, Hampden Park, OK, throw in Murrayfield as well – although we're convinced the SRU would arrange a series of friendlies against Botswana and some rock concerts at the same time just to spite us. But let's for argument's sake give them the benefit of the doubt. That still only adds up to four. We're still at least one, at most six, short.

Of course! We could lay some emotional blackmail on Barr Construction, get them to build some custom-built stadiums at prime locations all around the country so that everyone benefits – Oban, Rothesay, Wick, all big football towns. Then we could get them to upgrade a few of our existing stadiums. I mean, creating an extra 20,000 seats at the likes of Broadwood or Brockville shouldn't be a problem, and we could get them to do it free of charge or we'd spread it around that they don't love Scotland. OK, that's the stadium problem solved. Transport links could be the next wee hiccup.

See, that's another criterion UEFA insist on. A good transport infrastructure. Well, I suppose we could ask Brian Soutar to lay on some extra buses. As for the trains? Well, if they're sitting in the stations not going anywhere then I suppose they're keeping thousands of fans away from matches and thus reducing the chance of trouble. But would we even need transport in the first place? Scotland is a small country and I'm sure all true fans of the beautiful game would appreciate the beautiful countryside and wouldn't mind walking between venues because, after all, walking is good for you – just ask Gavin Hastings.

However, there could be one drawback. Now, call us naïve, but we thought if you wanted to make a bid for a football competition you would phone up the ruling body and say something like, 'Hello, this is Scotland, any chance a' hostin' your fitba' tourney n' that, know?' No way. Apparently it costs you something like a million quid to make a formal bid. Why a million pound? Well, all those expense-account meals, free holidays and fact-finding foreign junkets that our beloved SFA will have to get involved in if our bid is to be successful? Good luck lads, our hearts bleed for you.

WEDNESDAY, 28 JUNE

Settling down to watch the England/Romania match we were interested to see some of the celebs *and* ex-England players the camera picked out in the crowd. There was Sir Bobby Charlton looking, as usual, like he was ready to start crying – and that was *before* the match had even started – and we also saw Emlyn Hughes with, I don't know, his daughter maybe? His old Liverpool pal Mark Lawrenson was very reluctant to comment on it.

But even more interesting was the quick glimpse we caught of our own Shug Dallas sitting beside Pierluigi Collina. Now, there's a conversation we'd love to have eavesdropped on. What would they have been talking about? What things might Shuggie D. have been saying? Ever been skelped on the napper by a lire? Do you have much call for double-glazing in Italy? You ever heard of a guy call John Rowbotham? One thing's for sure, there's nothing Shug could say to raise Pierluigi's eyebrows – he doesn't have any.

THIS WEEK'S SPECIAL GUEST:

'CHICK YOUNG'

Ho! Ho! Ho! Totally sensational! Our own domestic season hasn't even started yet but already Europe and, dare I say it, yes I will, glory beckons for Scotland's totally superb Champions, the glorious Glasgow Rangers, even if they do face at the start of what will surely be a sensational campaign, what is known as a 'tricky' tie. 'Tricky' is a football journalistic term for, 'Our team should beat them but seeing as we don't really know what the opposition are like we'll hedge our bets slightly.'

The astonishing Teddy Bears face either a trip to Lithuania to face Zalgiris Kaunus – is that a football team or their entry for the *Eurovision Song Contest*? – or travel to Bosnia to play NK Brotnjo, that's pronounced 'Bront-yo', 'Brot-ne-jo' or' Bron-joe', depending on which radio station you listen to. Which of the two would Rangers prefer to play? They couldn't give a toss. Rangers could take both teams on at the same time and teach them a lesson in soccer slaughtery.

Now, I don't want to make any rash predictions but I reckon Rangers will go all the way and win the Champions League. I mean, come on. Surely, *surely* I am not going over the top, ranting like a loony or betraying my true colours when I say that a knighthood or a dukedom or an honorary captaincy in the Boys Brigade in the last Honours List would not have been out of line for the totally magnificent Mr Advocaat? Not only has he improved the quality of life for millions of people but he has also assembled a squad capable of crushing all before him as the mighty Sons of William sweep majestically towards world domination. *Eine* 'Gers! *Eine* coach! *Eine* people! Dutchman, Dutchman, *uber alles*! Thank you, I feel much better after that.

Right, that's all for now. Next week I'll be addressing the issue of too many foreigners in our game.

JULY 2000

SATURDAY, 1 JULY 2000

There was Rijkaard. The minute his team went out of Euro 2000, he held up his hands, declared himself a failure and nobly walked away from a job he loved. Portugal boss Humberto Coelho did exactly the same 24 hours earlier. In this country it's a different story. In this country the national managers hang on to their jobs like grim death. Why? Is it because of their dignity? Is it because they have a soccer vision that they dream of realising? No. We'll tell you why, it's because of the burds they can pull.

Now, we're not sure if Craig Brown takes a drink but he's obviously partial to a nice wee spot of Port – Louise Port, to be exact. He's only gone and nicked a chick nearly 200 years younger than himself. How does he do it? I mean, he's not exactly Brad Pitt, is he? Mind you, they say power is the greatest aphrodisiac of them all, but surely 'power' and 'Scotland boss' aren't words you would think of using in the same sentence? We have to say, though, we think this is nothing more than a holiday romance and it won't be long 'til wee Craigsie is on his bike – then, the next day, he'll leave Louise at the hotel and come back to Scotland.

SUNDAY, 2 JULY

Now there's a surprise. Dick Advocaat may have to start the season without the big-name striker Rangers have been promising the fans for months. There isn't a week goes by when the Scottish Champions aren't linked with some multi-million-pound hitman no one has ever heard of, and yet, here we are, six modest signings later and no expensive, overrated foreign dud in sight.

ONLY AN EXCUSE?

But before disgruntled Rangers fans start ripping up their Tina Turner tickets in protest, we can reveal just some of the names Rangers have been trying to lure to Ibrox.

RIPPOV: Russian striker currently with Moskow Drossko Under-21 Reserves. Valued at £16 million. Pounds or Embassy coupons? No one's sure.

NUNO TALENTO: Portuguese striker currently training with Luxembourg giants Kidjensen. Being chased by Benfica, Barcelona, Monaco. In fact, he has been chased by every club he's ever had a trial for. Current value £10 million o.n.o.

MANURO: known as the new Dunga. He's fat, lazy and extremely slow but he wears white boots so he must be good. Yours for just £7 million.

Take your pick.

MONDAY, 3 JULY

Ebbe Skovdahl was fairly dishing out the sour grapes last week. The man whose team should have been relegated but are now – by virtue of a woeful Cup Final appearance – in Europe, was having a right good whinge about Dick Advocaat buying up all the best young players, not just to strengthen Rangers but primarily to weaken the opposition. What about the moves Ebbe has taken to considerably strengthen *his* team? Hasn't he just gotten rid of Gary Smith? And once Gary signs on for a Scottish club, won't his presence in their defence considerably weaken that team? Come on, Ebbe, double standards or what?

TUESDAY, 4 JULY

Some people are calling Euro 2000 the 'greatest competition ever', so we suppose we should mark the end of a cracking football tournament. A quick word about the Semi-Finals.

The Holland/Italy match was all about penalties and when it came down to it Italy had their Totti while Holland had their Bosvelt – in more ways than one. Totti and his delicately chipped effort summed up just how confident Italy felt about the whole shoot-out scenario. What can you say about Holland in this match? Umpteen chances squandered, two missed penalties during the 90 minutes, three more during the shoot-out. If you're going to do that then there is a good chance you might not get through.

So the final itself, billed as not so much a game of football as progress versus the dirty, cheating, wasting, defensive Italians. Progress won but you couldn't help but feel for the Italians who, in the end, were just knackered both physically and mentally and were trying to take it to penalties so hell mend them.

Men of the match? Nesta. He's fair come on since he gave up packet meals to concentrate on football. Or was that Vesta? Zidane, that rarest of players, a balding one who doesn't shave his head. Cannavaro. Is he really Italian? Is he really an earthling? His eyebrows look distinctly Vulcan, couldn't he be Mr Spock's love child? Dugarry, a man whose face is like a magnet to the ball. Del Piero, whose finishing was more like Del Shannon.

'TOMMY BURNS'

Errr, this is very, very true. Everybody at Celticfootballclub has the best interests of Celticfootballclub at heart and, errr, sometimes in order to do good things you have to do bad things as well and Kenny Dalglish has had to leave the club. I feel for Kenny, the players feel for Kenny, Kenny feels for Kenny, but that's football. Everybody feels for each other. But, errr, it would also be very, very true to say that John Barnes was very, very wrong to say what he did when he didn't, but could have when he should have but chose not to.

This was very, very damaging for Celticfootballclub and I wouldn't like to apportion blame or point any fingers at anyone, but it was all his fault, so there. What does the future hold for Tommy Burns? Who can say? I'm just happy to be here, running through the glaur and dodging the dogs' jobbies in Strathclyde Park while Smarty Marty sits in the press lounge spouting his blarney. And I say that with no bitterness at all because that's football and I love it very, very dearly, especially at this time of year when traditionally Celticfootballclub have got their season ticket money in and are dragging their heels about signings.

I was really shocked, stunned, amazed, mortified when I heard what Chris Sutton's wife used to do for a living. I don't know how she can walk down the street or look in the mirror. No, I'm not talking about the nudey modelling, I'm talking about being a hostess on *Supermarket Sweep* with Dale Winton. That is just pure degrading, so it is.

But, errr, here we are, a new season beckons. You always know that the new season's coming soon because the wee red book comes out, the training gets harder and Phil O'Donnell's in the paper saying, 'All my injuries are behind me now and I'm raring to go.'

THURSDAY, 6 JULY

We've been asking around and we have to say we're having a tough time trying to find a Celtic fan who's genuinely excited about the arrival of Chris Sutton. Only a year ago a man as astute as Gianluca Vialli saw fit to fork out £10 million for the big striker and you don't suddenly become a diddy overnight, so he can't be that bad, can he? Maybe it's because the Hoops fans are still pining after Mark Viduka, who's currently having trouble securing a work permit – *work*, now there's a joke – so we reckon Sutton has to do something to prove he really does want to play for Celtic, something that shows he really is committed to the cause, something like *not* kissing the jersey when he scores.

Paul Gascoigne for Kilmarnock? Merely a rumour or merely a ridiculous rumour? There's never been any doubt about Gazza's ability or box-office draw, and another ex-Ranger would do the Killie fans just dandy. But is the Geordie Jehovah up to it any more? If Killie are looking for a drinking pal for Coisty and Durranty, why not go for someone with youth on their side and the potential to develop into a premier bevvy merchant. How about Euan Blair?

FRIDAY, 7 JULY

Don't know about you, but when we heard last week that the toaster from the Aberdeen dressing-room had been removed as part of an economy drive, we have to admit we were, to say the least, totally shocked. Aberdeen FC actually owned a toaster?

Admit it. There's nothing fans of one half of the Old Firm

love better than to see someone from the other half of the Old Firm being caught exposing their Sash or flashing their Catechism. We've all been to functions when things get out of hand. Much drink is usually swallied and yes, even famous former *Scotsport* presenters now with Sky can end up wearing Flute band jackets. But does that actually mean anything? So a Celtic rally in Las Vegas ended up with guys singing Irish Rebel songs? Surely not?

But what made this occasion so bad was that Celtic's chief executive had been there earlier and, during his speech, had referred to three members of his five-a-side team of 30 years ago as 'Huns'. What do you make of that, eh? Is that no' just terrible? Now, if Allan had been giving it laldy to some infamous Irish ditties like 'Kevin Barry', 'The Merry Ploughboy' or Johnny Logan's 'What's Another Year', then fair enough, get tore into him. But using the word 'Hun' hardly justifies a witch hunt. What Tim hasn't referred to his Protestant pal as a 'Hun'? What Hun hasn't referred to his Catholic pal as a 'Tim'? They have almost becomes terms of endearment. What Hun or Tim, in this day and age, truly cares about either of these names when there are so many other really offensive ones so freely available? As a great, great man once said, 'Bin this nonsense now.' So that's exactly what we're doing, binning *that* nonsense so that we can concentrate on some of the other nonsense happening with Celtic.

Let's start with matters on the park. Martin O'Neill got his first victory as Celtic manager thanks to a Tommy Johnson hat-trick as they overcame mighty Bray Wanderers 3–2. But seriously, though, what can you learn from these games? They're only training sessions played at a very sedate pace. In fact, the only tackle on the pitch was the set that belonged to the streaker.

Incidentally, Celtic went 1–0 down after a slip by Raphael – why do we feel that isn't the last time we'll hear that reported?

SUNDAY, 9 JULY

We don't mean to be 'ugly-ist', but with at least four of their new signings in the 'growler' class that fairly ups the hacket rating inside Ibrox Stadium. So I suppose that explains David Murray's move to tempt Brian Laudrup back – to improve the team photo. He may have had to pack in the game due to injury, but he can still pull a handsome coupon with the rest of them can Our Brian. Check out the front cover of the latest *Rangers News* for haddie-esque posing at its very best.

MONDAY, 10 JULY

First it was a Sheriff Court now it's a Carl Cort that could be signalling the end of the big time for Duncan Ferguson. Having signed Wimbledon's Carl Cort for £7 million, Newcastle United are now, allegedly, looking to off-load Duncan Do'nuts and reckon they might have trouble finding a buyer. Everybody is giving the rubber ear to a move for Dunky and we blame Rangers. The day they signed the big doo-fancier from Bannock-burn for the ridiculous fee of £4 million they created a monster. Although, in fairness, Frankenstein probably had less injuries in his career.

That £4 million fee hung like an albatross round Duncan's neck when a pigeon would have done. To say he's injury prone is like saying the world is round. He makes Phil O'Donnell look like the Bionic Man. But leaving aside the fact that he always seems to be injured, has anyone ever thought to ask the question, is he actually any good? His reputation seems to be built on one overhead kick against Germany which didn't actually find the net but somehow elevated him to the status of world-class striker. That, of course, is world class in a Scottish sense. And when you add up all the games Duncan has actually played, does it amount to one full season?

TUESDAY, 11 JULY

What a tawdry, mucky, sleazy, fascinating débâcle the dog-fight for the right to stage the 2006 World Cup Finals turned into. And what a surprise! Deutschland won it. We thought sure it would go to Germany. Seriously, though, could they lose? Making their case they had Franz Beckenbauer – the Kaiser, handsome, distinguished, articulate. And England? They've got Sir Bobby Charlton, moaning-faced Geordie, Geoff Hurst – why? – and Tony 'Rent a quote, invariably an ill-advised one' Banks with a bid that was along the lines of, 'We are England, so give us it now.' No chance.

But what about South Africa? – where the top-selling car accessory is a flame-thrower to ward off hi-jackers. They feel somebody did the dirty on them. They feel that minor issues such as lack of law and order and suitable stadiums should have been overlooked in awarding them the Finals.

Every sleazy drama needs a baddie and one conveniently emerged, New Zealand's very own Charlie Dempsey. Can we just say that what he did was shocking, shameful and he should never be forgiven for it. No, not welching on his promise to back South Africa, voting for England in the first round.

'CRAIG BROWN'

Ehhh weeelll, what a busy few days I've had, let me tell you. I'm feeling quite exhausted – but enough about me and Louise Port. What else have I been up to? Well, I went to the national stadium to see Tina Turner. I felt quite at home in that environment – being the Scotland boss I'm used to seeing old has-beens doddering about Hampden. Then I was off to Holyrood for a blether with an old friend of mine, Phil the Greek. It was most pleasant. Phil showed his total grasp of the situation and understanding of who I was by asking me about cricket. 'How are the googlies?' he asked. 'Still in perfect working order,' I advised him most proudly.

I was sorry I hadn't been able to make it the previous day when Phil's missus was dishing out gongs. Sean Connery got his knighthood, although to be honest I was quite surprised because yes, Big Tam wore a kilt but no, it wasn't the Rangers tartan. Was I jealous of Sean? Weeelll, ehhh, I can say quite categorically that I am not. A knighthood would be very nice and I know many people in football have their OBEs and the MBEs, but given all the recent publicity I've been receiving about my love life, I'm more than happy with my OJS – that's Order of the Jammy So-and-so.

You know, it really is pretty tough when an old … err, I mean … a mature man such as myself is winching strong with such a young, energetic, foxy burd like the one I've managed to lumber. It's like Christmas Day and your birthday all rolled into one every morning. But I know that soon I'm going to have to put love on hold and concentrate on the job in hand, getting Scotland into the World Cup. And rest assured, I'm still taking that task very seriously indeed, and I can further assure you that I will continue to approach my work in a mature and sensible manner.

Now, if you'll excuse me, I'm just away to an S Club 7 gig.

ONLY AN EXCUSE?

MONDAY, 17 JULY

Mikey Mols, the striker with the Metz Judderman hairstyle, has been quietly working on his injured knee, rebuilding it day by day so that it'll be completely ready for its next long-term injury. Rumours had it that Molsy's knee was still giving him problems but he's been knocking them in against top-class third-rate opposition like Quick Twente, whose defence were more like Quick Hide, on Rangers' pre-season tour. But let's be honest. He could play in Scotland with one leg and still score 20 goals a season.

New boy Fernando Ricksen seems to fancy himself as a bit of a wide boy. A hard man who likes to 'play rough' and is 'impossible to control', just who have the Sons signed here, Steven Segal? The big Dutchman says he hopes that the Scottish referees will allow him to 'play his game' – in other words, allow him to get away with murder. Don't worry, Nando, in *that* jersey you'll have no problems at all.

TUESDAY, 18 JULY

Well, it certainly didn't take Celtic's record signing, Chris Sutton, long to make all the wrong headlines, did it? The past caught up with him last week when he got done good and proper for spitting at a lawyer. Now, OK, we know it was a lawyer and we've probably all felt like having a swing at a member of that profession at least once in our lives. But while a punch, a kick or a nutting are still revered as a way of settling an argument in these parts, the same cannot be said for the ignoble art of lobbing a gob at your adversary.

Now, let's get one thing straight here. Spitting is a vile and disgusting habit, but surely only when the grogger itself is directed at someone. The casual ejaculation of phlegm from the gub is at worst harmless, at best an exhibition of performance art. Today's professional footballer, however, has turned spitting into the ultimate insult that can be bestowed upon an opponent. Take Mark Viduka – ironically the man Sutton replaced at Celtic Park – another spitter of some infamy. In a fit of pique, the big Aussie fired one at Dunfermline's Marc Miller. Viduka claimed he didn't see Miller as the Pars player was wearing black and white vertical stripes which, like a zebra, gave him excellent camouflage. But the ref would hear none of it and a red card was shown.

Viduka had let himself down. I mean, if you're going to spit, you're going to get sent off so you might as well make it a right, good grogger and make sure you hit the guy square on the coupon. Viduka's effort was watery and inaccurate and a disgrace to his profession.

'CHARLIE NICHOLAS'

Indefinitely so, Paul Gascoigne has skill in abundancy and rightly so. His ability alone speaks volumes for itself in spades. He is beyond a shadow of a question top drawer of the quality tree. An immensely talented individual thanks in no small measure to his talent. At Rangers he was good but only in a Rangersly way. His return to the English football of England exposed a lackness of other important things. His armoury was no longer in his arsenal, and fitness was now the issue, which is ironical. In Scotland you don't need to be fit, all you need is natural skill in plentiness, a good head on your brain, and elbows. I like elbows. Elbows is good and crucially so. Anatomy-wise, not only do they make your arms bend, but they enable fat blokes to run about football pitches and breenge opponents out the way, which is latterly, towards the end, what Gascoigne was prone to do. And why not, he got away with it. Which is ironical. Gascoigne's surprise move to Middlesbrough was no shock to anyone who didn't know him. As a Geordie he couldn't resist the lure of Teesside. He had nothing to prove except for everything and he didn't. Even his elbows let him down when he managed to break his own arm with an ill-informed swing at an opponent. Now he's back and by all accounts looking great, otherwise why would Middlesbrough be willing to pay half his wages for him to go away and play somewhere else? Questions have arisen about coming back to Scotland, but this for me is questionable.

Comebacks can be regrettable and dangerously so. The mongers in the rumour factory are rumour-wise already spreading gossip over the big man's future. Motherwell were interested in spades as were Kilmarnock, who undeniably denied it. Kilmarnockally speaking, I think it would be a big gamble of some risk. To bring Paul Gascoigne back to Scotland would be an enormous toss of the dices.

SATURDAY, 22 JULY

In recent times there has been a misguided sense of 'this time we're gonnae dae it' among the fans at Celtic Park based on nothing more than blind optimism. It was never more to the fore than the day the Barnes/Dalglish dream ticket appointment was made, and look how all that ended.

This time it's totally different. Under the pragmatic O'Neill, Celtic have reverted to the 'reality check' philosophy championed by their former president, Fergus McCann, and it seems to be working. Celtic fans have cast aside daft ideas of instant glory and are getting to grips with the fact that, if they are going to see their team beat Rangers, it's going to be a long, long haul.

However, patience is not something you buy by the carrierbag load out of the Celtic Superstore on match days, and the question is, how much longer will the fans bear with O'Neill's realistic approach to what lies ahead as long as guys like Raphael and Tebily are in the team? At least with them on the park, Alan Stubbs knows what it's like playing with a pair of goolies again.

In fairness, Stubbs has been more than understanding about the performances of Raphael and Tebily. Stubbsy claims it can't be easy for them, given they don't speak very good English. Well, neither does Stubbs and he manages. Anyway, what part of the phrases, 'Man on', 'Clear it' and 'Nawwww!!!' don't Raphael and Tebily understand?

SUNDAY, 23 JULY

We can't put a finger on it but we somehow get the feeling that there's something not quite right with Rangers. Six, or was it seven, or was it eight, nine even – whatever number of summer signings, a first-team squad of around 75 players and yet are we sniffing the first whiff of internal conflict coming from within Castle Greyskull? There are just too many Rangers players falling over themselves to come out and say how happy they are to stay and fight for their place, and how much The Gaffer has helped them become better players.

But as far as real news goes there's a distinct lack of action. For example, just what is the situation regarding Mikey Mols' knee. Any truth in the rumour that Rangers are seriously concerned because the knee has swollen so badly that Mols can't roll up his trouser leg to attend club meetings? And just what is going on with Lorenzo Amoruso? What is the big Italian's future at Rangers? Is The Gaffer restructuring his side, or is wee Dick simply making a Konterman of Big Amo? And how about that shock defeat by Livingston? Mind you, what are friendlies and what can they tell you? Well, with Rangers, friendlies are valuable when they're winning them and just part of the build-up when they lose them. But a defeat is a defeat and not what you're hoping for before you start another European campaign. Incidentally, on the 'we're definitely going to make a big signing' front we can exclusively reveal that David Murray is *not* about to sign up Tiger Woods as a golf buddie for his pal 'Big Tam' Connery.

MONDAY, 24 JULY

How long did you think Hernan Crespo's world-record transfer fee of £35.5 million was actually going to remain the world-record transfer fee? Not long, we thought. No sooner had the crayon dried on Crespo's contract than Fiorentina claimed they had already turned down an offer of £40 million for their goalkeeper Francesco Toldo. £40 million! For a goalie!?!? AC Milan have already said they would be prepared to pay £40 million for a player, which kind of puts the Scottish record transfer fee of a piddly wee £6 million into perspective.

So, what kind of player are AC Milan talking about here? Inzhagi? Rivaldo? Barry Ferguson? Wrong. Milan are said to be snoaching around David Beckham and persistently waving a £40 million wad under Sir Fergie's nose. I suppose with someone like Beckham money isn't going to go to his head because he's already loaded. Mind you, this is partly because his wife works too.

With the wages they can earn and the cars they drive and the model burds they pull and the fights they get into, footballers are, these days, being compared to movie stars. But the thing is, signing up a film star is much less of a risk than buying a footballer. You see, no matter how rotten the film might turn out to be the star will be in it, even if they die during the making of it. Check out Ollie Reed in *Gladiator*. There are, however, no such special effects available that can put a crock on the pitch or, indeed, make a haddie look like a player.

So, what are we saying about the overblown state of the transfer market? We're saying it's time clubs stopped paying out ridiculous amounts for guys who are more likely to damage a cruciate ligament while dancing the 'Macarena' in Scamps Disco than through their efforts on the field of play, and start paying ridiculous amounts for Hollywood superstars instead. Just think if you had Geordie Clooney or Tam Cruise or Bradzo Pitt in your line-up? Everybody would turn up just to look at them and it wouldn't matter if they were useless. They're actors, you could hire a stunt man to do all the football bits for them.

ONLY AN EXCUSE?

Controversial? Perhaps. Daft? Of course, but we say, why pay footballers to behave like pampered superstars when, for less money, you could get the real thing? Anyway, £35.5 million? Old hat. Real Madrid have just forked out £37 million for Barcelona's really quite good Portuguese star, Luis Figo. So, how long do you think this world-record transfer fee will remain the world-record transfer fee?

WEDNESDAY, 26 JULY

Predictions? Well, we don't normally like to make predictions until after the event but, OK then, seeing as the start of the new season is looming, and seeing as it's sort of traditional at this time, and seeing as everyone else is doing it, we'll have a go as well.

Premier Championship (the first bit): Rangers
Premier Championship (the second bit): Rangers
Scottish Cup: Rangers
League Cup: Rangers
Davis Cup: Rangers
The Ashes: Rangers
Eurovision Song Contest: Celtic (well, Ireland)
Stars In Your Eyes Final: Rangers (as Larkhall Flute Band)
Player of the Year: Barry Ferguson
Young Player of the Year: Barry Ferguson
Sportscene Personality of the Year: Barry Ferguson
New Leader of the SNP: Barry Ferguson
New President of the USA: Dick Advocaat
Nobel Prize for Literature: *Only an Excuse?*

'JIM WHITE'

Hi, I'm here with a round-up of all the latest news that, to be honest, I couldn't give a toss about. First up, what about St Mirren, 'The Buddies', Chick Young's team – only kidding, Chico. Wee bit of inter-pundit banter there. Well, in the race to snap up José Quitongo I'm afraid it's bad news for the Paisley side. They won it and José is now a St Mirren player. No luck there.

And what about Hibs? – who, incidentally, I must thank for discovering Kenny Miller for Rangers. Their very own Russell Latapy only scored the winning goal for his country against Mexico in a World Cup qualifier. The question I'm asking, though, is this one. How come Trinidad *and* Tobago are allowed to join up and kid on they're only one country? That's not fair, unless, of course, Scotland and Brazil or Holland or Italy were able to join up, then it would be great.

A wee bit of sad news now. Apparently Partick Thistle's new Albanian trialist goalie, Luljan Gjloshi, has been having a bit of a jittery time. But I feel that once he settles in he'll be fine. After all, from Albania to Firhill, that's a hell of a shock for anyone to take.

What about Tiger Woods? Isn't it terrible when one guy dominates a sport – apart, of course, from Scottish football. Dick Advocaat, what a character. Rangers, what a team full of characters. David Murray, what a god. Blue, what a colour. Orange, what a colour as well. The new away strip, what a fashion statement. Ibrox, what a temple. As for their oldest rivals *them*, the Beggars, Celtic. Will they do anything this season or will they struggle once again to keep up with their rightful masters, the glorious 'Gers? Well, speaking as a neutral I just want whatever's best for the game – aye, that'll be right.

Cheers mates, catch you later.

ONLY AN EXCUSE?

FRIDAY, 28 JULY

It is one of the great traditions of Scottish football journalism, trying to be the pundit who comes up with the definitive pronunciation of a foreigner's name. In this case it's Celtic's brand-new Belgian, Joos Valgaeren who's causing all the problems. So far we've heard him called 'Yowse', 'Jo-uus', 'Joosh', 'Yoss', 'Joze' and 'Yooooooooz'. His surname is causing a few problems too. 'Val-Haeren', 'Valccchherrren', 'Valhalla', 'Valsingleton'. You'd think that at the press conference, before they ask such probing questions as, 'Why did you join Celtic?' and, 'Do you like Scotland?', somebody would have the gumption or bottle even to bite the bullet and just come out with it. 'Hey, big man, gonnae tell us how to say your name?'

Now unfortunately, we cannot shed any more light on the subject of how to pronounce 'Yowse', 'Jo-uus', 'Joosh', 'Yoss', 'Joze' or 'Yooooooooz's name but we can exclusively reveal what 'Valgaeren' actually means. It's an old Flemish word meaning, 'better than Tebily and Raphael'.

MONDAY, 31 JULY

We felt for Antii Niemi on Sunday. It can't have been much fun being hit by a plastic cup of Bovril. Still, it could have been worse. At least it's traditional at Scottish grounds to always sell Bovril cold, so at least there was no chance of the keeper being scalded.

Start of a new season of football, start of a new season of sports broadcasting of the very highest standard. What a weekend it was. Did anyone happen to catch last Friday night's meeting of *Lodge Sportscene*? From Ibrox Stadium it came, there's a surprise, eh? Ah well, start as you mean to go on. We wonder how many more *Friday Night Sportscenes* will be broadcast direct from the Mother Lodge, how many exclusive interviews Dick Advocaat gives about nothing in particular, how many exclusive interviews David Murray gives on how much money his club has, and how many exclusive interviews with ex-Rangers personalities like Walter Smith and Paul Gascoigne there'll be.

The following day it was radio's turn. *Sportsound* v. *Scoreboard*. The Old Infirmed of Scottish radio broadcasting. Throughout the season – on an almost weekly basis – we can look forward to both programmes claiming that official figures conclusively prove they are now the most listened-to, and therefore the fans favourite, football programme. Of course, which one you prefer is really down to which station has the pundits you can't stand the least. But generally speaking, there's little to choose between the two as both proved on their big 'opening day of the season' shows on Saturday. Both stations had riveting interviews with Roger 'Harry Potter' Mitchell on the fascinating subject of League reconstruction. Ho'd me back. There was also a choice of match commentaries: Rangers v. St Johnstone or Rangers v. St Johnstone. It was a difficult choice but in the end we stuck with Clyde and their commentary team of Dougie MacDonald with Derek Johnstone and Mark Hateley simply because we just felt that, with them, we'd be guaranteed unbiased, objective coverage.

On Saturday night we had *Sportscene Match of the Day* with its interesting new titles in which, between predictable footie clips, they flash up subliminal, satanic messages – no kiddin', we taped it and slowed it down – saying things like, 'All bow before Advocaat the one true god', and, 'The mark of the beast is on all those who follow the Teddy Bears'. STV hadn't just been standing by all this time, though. There was *Scotsport Extra Time* on Saturday with Jim Delahunt, *Scotsport* on Sunday afternoon with Jim Delahunt, *Scotsport* on Sunday night with Jim Delahunt and, in case you weren't getting enough in-depth football analysis, there was a special feature on their news and current affairs magazine, *Seven Days* – just after *Scotsport* on Sunday afternoon – in which Bernard Ponsonby interviewed Iain McCall and – yes, you guessed it – Jim Delahunt. In fact, the only Scottish production J.D. wasn't in over the weekend was *Taggart*.

Of course, in the midst of all this we've got ever-dependable Sky Sports, with Jim and Charlie. What a pair of characters. On Sunday Charlie managed to come up with a new geometry term, the 'diangle', and a new concept in soccer punditry – insisting on waiting until half-time before making any predications as to the outcome of the match, while Jim sat with the bemused look on his face of a kid whose mind was only on two things: 'When will this be finished?' and, 'I wonder what's in my "play piece"?'. Fantastical stuff and rightly so in spades.

AUGUST 2000

'WALTER SMITH'

Well, obviously, particularly, at the present moment our season hasn't started down here so we're just enjoying some nice, friendly matches like the one last week with Graeme Souness's Blackburn Rovers. There was a slight misunderstanding on the pitch which led to a bit of a disagreement amongst some of the players. but obviously the newspapers blew it all out of proportion. They were saying there were 12 players involved in a mass brawl but that was just ridiculous. You can take it from me, there were only 11.

Obviously, at the present moment, I still keep an eye on what's happening back home *and* at places outside Ibrox Stadium too. I hear Aberdeen are still in the grubber and need their finances sorted out. So, what's the problem? Don't they get those Carol Vorderman 'First Plus' adverts in the Grampian region? She'll sort them out.

At the present moment a lot of attention is on Celtic. I saw them play against Dundee United who looked obviously odd in their green shirts. Would never have happened in my day. I sometimes wonder why United just don't go the full hog and get back to calling themselves Dundee Hibernians. They always lie down to Celtic anyway. Celtic looked, I have to say, quite not bad and could be strengthened further this week with the arrival of Mark Bosnich. This, I feel, would be a further move towards bringing together the Old Firm divide. The Celtic fans will love him because he's a top-class goalkeeper and the Rangers fans would love him because he once gave a Nazi salute.

Sadly, things seem to be going well for the Beggars but I still have a question that I hope Martin O'Neill can answer for me. Just what *does* Stephane Bonnes look like? Do they still have that wee guy, Regi Blinker, playing for them? What a laugh we used to have down at the Palace when we were watching the Old Firm match on the Royal telly and Celtic would bring him on as substitute. What a wheeze.

FRIDAY, 4 AUGUST 2000

Apologies to Regi Blinker. We were poised to announce he was back in Holland negotiating a deal to be an ice-cream man but actually it's *Den Haag* he's having talks with and not as, we first thought, *Hagen Daas*.

MONDAY, 7 AUGUST

In the euphoria that surrounded the start of our own domestic season we almost missed out on two very interesting European matches last week. In the Inter Toto Cup – a competition sponsored by Toto, the American AOR band that had hits with 'Hold the Line' and 'Africa' – we witnessed quite possibly the worst refereeing performance of all time from the aptly named Mr Schoch from Switzerland. Celtic fans please note. 'Schoch' is *not* the German for 'Dallas'. We also had Steve Stone taking the sole of a boot, full force on his face – luckily the boot wasn't too badly damaged – which resulted in so much blood we thought Villa had sacked John Gregory and brought in Sam Peckinpah as a replacement.

Then there was the Inter Milan/Juventus match for a trophy that looked like a Bird's Eye Waffle having to be settled not by penalties but by a shoot-out. From about 30 metres out the player has seven seconds to run in on goal and score. The keeper can come off his line. Out of ten attempts only three hit the net, and for one of the goals the outfield player took longer than the regulation seven seconds. Inter Milan's Robbie Keane was actually brought down by the goalie as he prepared to shoot. A penalty? No, he was made to do the whole run-in thing all over again.

A keepie-uppie competition, head tennis, seeing who can pee the highest against the wall, they've all got to be better ways to decide a final than the farce of the shoot-out. Bin this nonsense now, you know it makes sense.

We don't know what Juan Sara is playing at but somebody should tell him that religion is only supposed to be a West of Scotland issue. But clearly Juan Sara upped the ante down Tayside way when he upped the jersey to reveal a 'Jesus Loves You' tee-shirt as part of his goal-scoring celebration. The player obviously doesn't realise the kind of country he's living in so probably didn't realise he just can't flash a slogan like that without qualifying whether he meant a 'Protestant' Jesus or a 'Catholic' Jesus?

TUESDAY, 8 AUGUST

Ibrox in crisis? Is the once-mighty Rangers empire starting to crumble? Have the team lost their gladiatorial spirit? Are cracks appearing in the ramparts of Castle Greyskull? Is it just us or is Dick Advocaat not quite himself lately?

In fairness to The Gaffer – as most of the Scottish media like to call him – life for Dick Advocaat at Ibrox Stadium must be like being in Channel Four's *Big Brother*, with film crews following him everywhere and footie journos hanging on to every word. As manager of the Scottish Champions, who just so happen to be Rangers, he is constantly under the spotlight. In fact, Carol Vorderman's been complaining that he gets too much coverage.

Maybe that's why we feel he seems more crabit these days. Preoccupied, confused, he's started wearing brown shoes with black trousers. Surely in direct defiance of Rangers' stringent dress code? Why is his team struggling? Why can't Rangers sign a top-class striker? What's going to happen when they start playing real teams in Europe?

'He's off in two years,' says one report. 'No, he's not,' says another. Now there's talk of him staying on at the club as some sort of President of Everything. Mmm, President Advocaat. Maybe the Scottish Parliament could all wear Orange that day as a tribute to what he's done for the country?

One very interesting footnote to Saturday's match. Apparently, there was a bit of trouble when police discovered Rangers supporters in amongst the Kilmarnock supporters. How could they tell the difference?

'FERGUS McCANN'

You know, that's the sad thing about being a tax exile, you have to leave behind dear old Bonnie Scotland and live in a country where the sun always shines. The other sad thing is that you miss out on great occasions like the Queen Mum's birthday celebrations. I can just imagine all those thousands of street parties breaking out all over Larkhall. You know, she's a very rich woman, the Queen Mother, almost as rich as me, so you'd think with all that money and with her 100th birthday coming up, she might have paid a visit to the dentist. A wee polish to the gnashers wouldn't have gone amiss.

But, you know, I do miss Scotland, which is such a wonderful if somewhat bizarre place. I mean, where else in the world could you find Robbie Williams, Geri Halliwell *and* Chick Young all on the front page of a daily newspaper?

And people still come up to me and ask me about Celtic and about the time Mr Ken Dalglish, Mr James Kerr and Mr The Other Bloke tried to take over my club. I thought something smelled fishy about them at the time and I was right because Mr Kerr then went on to open a sushi bar. Incidentally, I won't be visiting Mr Kerr's sushi bar. I've had enough haddies to last me a lifetime.

I've recently heard a showbiz rumour they are going to make a movie about Burns with Johnny Depp in the starring role. Now, I know my eyesight is that wee bit dodgy but Johnny Depp looks nothing like Tommy Burns.

By the way, I was watching *Sportscene Match of the Day* the other night and, I don't know, I could be wrong, but do you think they used enough red, white and blue in the studio set? I mean, perish the thought, but one could come away with the idea that a slight bias existed at the BBC.

Now, if you'll excuse me, I'm off to count thin dimes and smell some coffee.

ONLY AN EXCUSE?

FRIDAY, 11 AUGUST

It didn't take Ken Bates long to get tore into Chris Sutton, did it? From the safety of Stamford Bridge the controversial – i.e. big-mouthed – Chelsea Führer labelled his former player 'a disaster'. Well, I suppose that's one way of looking at it. Another is that Sutton's goal-scoring ratio at Chelsea was once every three games which a lot of strikers would be quite happy with.

One other thing regarding Master Bates. It concerns Sir Alex Ferguson. Apparently, after the Charity Shield match, Bates tried to hang a winner's medal around Sir Alex's neck and Fergie nudged him away. This is nothing short of pathetic, *nudging* him away, come on, Fergie, you're a Govan boy, you should have done us all a favour and given him the double Malky.

SATURDAY, 12 AUGUST

To quote Big Billy Shakespeare's *Romeo and the Burd*, 'What's in a name? That which we call a Breakaway League, by any other name would still smell.' A breakaway league – and we're not talking a league sponsored by a company that makes the chocolate biscuit – now seems to be a certainty. Roger 'Harry Potter' Mitchell and his equivalents from Holland, Belgium and Portugal – plus the bloke who represents their equivalents in Norway, Denmark, Sweden and Finland who will all be lumped together as Scandinavia – have been locked in secret talks that everybody seems to have known about for months and now it's official. Purely for the good of the game, the Old Firm, plus whoever the third force in Scottish football happens to be at the time, will be off to play in this new version of the Atlantic League while the rest of Scottish football will be left to play in the Loch Lomond League.

So, just what are the facts behind this, the biggest revolution to hit Scottish football since they stopped using cast-iron footballs in 1895? Do they sell macaroon bars at European grounds? Can we learn how to shout abuse at players in Dutch, Flemish, Portuguese and Scandish in time? Will we have to pay for our season tickets in Euros? We managed to track down a very important insider with the SPL and he agreed to provide the answers to the questions that no one is remotely interested in asking.

QUESTION: Just what is Roger Mitchell's brief at the SPL?
ANSWER: It's Roger's job to take pelters from Hugh Keevins and Jim Traynor every week on Radio Clyde.

QUESTION: Why is this breakaway league different from previous breakaway leagues?
ANSWER: Because it has been approved by UEFA, FIFA, SPL, MFI, TGIF etc. So it's not a breakaway league, it's a runaway-with-the-money league.

QUESTION: Will it be any better than what we already have?
ANSWER: Yes, because of the quality of the opposition. From Holland the likes of Ajax and PSV, from Scandinavia the likes of Brondby and Herfolge.

QUESTION: How come there's no teams from France, Spain, Germany or Luxembourg? Aren't our teams just entering a second-division television league?
ANSWER: How come you're so negative? You're starting to get on my tits.

QUESTION: What about the Scottish Cup?
ANSWER: Ah, I'm glad you asked me that. Both the Old Firm will

continue to play in the Cup so Scottish referees won't have to abandon biased refereeing completely.

QUESTION: Without the Old Firm won't this make winning the Scottish Premier League like winning the First Division?
ANSWER: Aye. So?

QUESTION: So, wasn't the last round of League reconstruction a complete waste of time?
ANSWER: You got a problem with that?

MONDAY, 14 AUGUST

Bit of a PR *faux pas* that from Celtic, was it not? Allan MacDonald breaks cover after weeks of low profile bordering on invisibility, and what's the first thing he says to the fans? 'Gie' us mair money.' And we're not just talking 10p for a cup of tea. Celtic are millions in debt – hold on, what was that? Sorry, we thought we could hear the voice of Fergus McCann on the wind saying, 'I told you so' – and still to settle financially with the Barnes/Dalglish dream team.

But the big question being kicked around at the moment is an old one. Who actually watched Raphael before Celtic parted with the £5 million? This has come to the fore again following allegations that a secret agent had received a considerable fee for his involvement in the deal. Who was this agent and who was he working on behalf of? Rangers, perhaps? Supposedly Celtic did watch a video of Raphael. Well, it must must have been made by George Lucas' Dreamworks Studio because only the very latest in computer-generated visual effects could make this guy look like a player. Anyway, we should all learn a wee bit more following the Celtic AGM – Still, for our money, the best soap opera around.

'PAUL GASCOIGNE'

Way aye, man! I'm really happy to be back playin' with Wolt-ah again. When I was up at Rangers Wolt-ah was great for me, he really was. In fact, I'd go as far as to say Wolt-ah was like a manager to me. He really was. And I'm so happy to hear that Wolt-ah is hoping to bring Big Duncan Ferguson back to Everton 'cos he's a good lad is big Dunc and me and him have so much in common. He likes pigeons, I like fishing — as I said, so much in common. And I'm sure, now that I'm much more sensible, Wolt-ah will be wanting me to look out for Duncan, keep an eye on him, make sure he doesn't get into trouble.

By the way, what about that William Hague, eh? Says when he was a lad he used to drink 14 pints a day. Fourteen pints. What a wimp! If you're only drinking 14 pints a day you should be seeing a doctor to find out what's wrong with you.

And I see my old mate Andy Goram's getting married. *Hello, Hello* magazine are doing the pictures. I must ask Wolt-ah if I can have a week off for the stag night.

But, hey, listen. What's this with the Dundee player and his tee-shirt saying 'Jesus Loves You'? How can he say that? That's just daft, that is. I mean, I've never even met Jesus Sanjuan of Airdrie so how can he love me? I wonder if he loves Roy Keane as well? Listen, didn't Roy do well on Sunday? That stress counselling he's been receiving is obviously working a treat. It took a full 61 minutes before he took his crucial maddie.

Before I go, congratulations to Andy McLaren of Kilmarnock for his superb start to the season. The lad's come through a lot, so well done to him. I must remember to send him a crate of champagne.

ONLY AN EXCUSE?

MONDAY, 21 AUGUST

I suppose with a big week in Europe coming up we should have something of a European preview. But let's be honest, could you be bothered to read it because we can't be bothered to write it. Even given Scotland's legendary ability to snatch defeat from the jaws of victory, we can't see there being even the remotest whiff of upset which means Rangers, Celtic, Hearts and Bohemians will all go through. If Aberdeen were to rally and make it to the next leg then that would be a shock result. OK, it's only highlights we're seeing on television – *high*lights, now there's a laugh – but even allowing for bad luck, the run of the ball, the bounce of the ball, more bad luck and a team full of diddies, Aberdeen look even more dispirited than they did last season when somehow they managed to reach two Cup Finals, one of which saw them qualify for European humiliation. The only thing you could say for the Dandy Dons is at least they have a candidate for the 'save of the season'. Just a pity it was Mark Perry who made it.

Skovdahl. So laid back he's practically horizontal. Wandering around Pittodrie like some old hippy still dreaming of Woodstock. Nothing seems to bother this character, absolutely nothing at all. With all the drive of a man seeing out a lucrative contract who knows after this one he'll never work again. I bet Dons fans never thought they'd see the day they'd look back and smile as they dreamed of the golden era of Roy Aitken.

TUESDAY, 22 AUGUST

Fan power. That was the buzz phrase last week, all because of some new charter they've brought out down South to make sure football fans get a good deal. We'll see how long that lasts.

In Scotland we've known for years that fans get a raw deal. After all, what do you expect? We live in rip-off Britain, where everything is a lower quality and a higher price than anywhere else in the world. We don't think the product in this country is perfect, nor do we think we get value for wur dosh. But let's make sure our comparisons with other countries are accurate before we start putting our game down. When we see lists comparing the price of some item in this country with a similar item in another, the 'facts' can be deceptive.

For example, they quote maybe £2 for a burger and chips and £1.20 for a drink. But who actually has only the one can after a burger and chips at a football match? There is usually so much salt in the burger and chips you need at least three cans of juice to wash it all down. So are our matches actually much dearer than comparable matches in, for example, Spain or Holland? No. OK, it might cost a mere £282 for a season ticket for Barcelona, but this does not take into account hidden extras, like how much it costs for the wee boys who say, 'Can I watch your motor mister?' Here we give them what, a quid? 50p? In Spain it's £100 or they bring in a low-loader and ship your car out to the Far East.

'DENIS LAW'

Well, you know, as I say, it's not often I make the headlines any more these days. But I managed it last week with those chancers from a sports company using the names of Denis Law, Archie Gemmill and Joe Jordan in their advertising campaign. At first I thought, now that's a bit of a coincidence, some guy has got the exact same name as me. Then I thought, hold on, it *is* me.

What a bunch of cheeky besoms, eh? I tell you, see when I first saw the sign, I was shocked. It would have made my hair stand on end but for the fact that my hair always stands on end anyway. 'Denis Law to resume playing career.' That's what it said, 'Denis Law to resume playing career.' Soon as I read it I thought, 'Oh no, don't tell me Turino want me to come back and see out my contract,' but no, turns out it's not true, it's a wind-up, a joke. Apparently I'm not making a comeback after all.

To be honest, I'll bet you there are a lot of people upset that I'm not really making a comeback. Isn't Dick Advocaat still looking for a world-class striker? Well, here's one with the reactions of a mongoose just waiting for the call. I said to my agent, 'What would be my transfer fee?' He said, 'Nothing.' I said, 'don't be ridiculous. This is the Lawman we're talking about. I must be worth at least £20 million.' He said, 'Bosman,' I said, 'No, it's absolutely true.'

Incidentally, viewers of Manchester United/Newcastle United on Sky might have seen those legendary Manchester United legends Sir Bobby, Bestie and yours truly at half-time, on the pitch, receiving awards for, well, basically for being legendary Manchester United legends Sir Bobby, Bestie and yours truly, I suppose. They were given to us by yet another soccer legend, the big Portuguese legend from Spain, I think, Hugh Sabio. Somebody mentioned Ben Fica as well, but I never saw him there.

FRIDAY, 25 AUGUST

You may remember a while back we posed the question, is there enough red, white and blue on show in the *Lodge Sportscene* set? Well, did we get a shock on Saturday, or what? Not only were the reds, whites and blues bolder than ever but we had a huge splash of orange too. Now we're not advocating a total shift in colour scheme to something – shall we call it for argument's sake – more neutral. We're just suggesting that Dougie Donnelly tones down the shade of his hair dye.

SATURDAY, 26 AUGUST

If you're still not sure about an alleged blue-nose bias emanating from Queen Margaret Drive then what about the punter who confronted one of us just this week with what can only be described as conclusive proof. The man – let's call him Jimmy X, because his first name is Jimmy and he can't spell his second name – approached and said, 'Hey, ho, you're those b*******ds out the papers, aren't you? Well, put this in your column. See last Friday, thon Hazel Walker said on *Reporting Scotland* that Hibs were one point ahead of Rangers. They were actually one point ahead of Rangers *and* Celtic. So, what does that tell you, eh? Put that in your column, go'on, ah dare you.' Well, Jimmy, dare accepted. Proof that we are prepared to go out on a limb just to make sure our readers get the facts.

MONDAY, 28 AUGUST

In recent years there has been a pattern of Old Firm matches. Rangers keep it tight at the back, soak up the pressure, hit Celtic on the break. Well, in this first Judgement Day of the

new season, keeping it tight was exactly what Rangers did –
for the first 50 seconds. Within 12 minutes the 'Gers were three
down and their tormentor in chief was Bobby Petta – the man
with a name that sounds like a sex aid – who turned Fernando
Ricksen – the Rangers Raphael? – inside out. Never one to sit
back and watch one of his players having a shocker, Advocaat
acted quickly and pulled Ricksen off after 20 minutes, much to
the relief of the shell-shocked Rangers fans and indeed Ricksen
himself. Have you ever seen anyone so relieved to be substituted
in your life?

Three–nil up and coasting, Celtic sat back and Rangers came
more and more into the game. Tugay – whose hairstyle is rapidly
getting close to a mullett – was making a difference and perhaps
it was no surprise when a Rod Wallace cross was met by Claudio
Reyna and Rangers were back in the match. Critics of Jonathan
Gould say he was at fault, but we're not so sure. Had the Celtic
keeper come for the ball, he might have clutched Reyna's head by
mistake. You mean, you hadn't noticed that Rangers' American
beauty has a head shaped like a bowling ball?

A minute later it looked as though Rangers had pulled another
goal back when Rod Wallace stuck one away, but it was ruled
off-side. Television replays showed that the assistant referee had
got it wrong – or had he? If he had allowed play to continue
then Mahe would have kept going and clattered Wallace a full
two seconds after the striker had put the ball into the net, been
red-carded, took a maddie and refused to go off, started a riot,
Celtic would have lost the plot and Rangers would have won
4–3. So, perhaps common sense prevailed. Anyway, this decision
should go a long way towards curing the Celtic faithful of any
paranoia over anti-Fenian flag men – until, at least, the next Old
Firm match.

TUESDAY, 29 AUGUST

I don't know if anyone noticed, but the other week Auchinleck Talbot played Cumnock and, sadly, yet again, what a huge disappointment this proved to be because, well, nothing happened. No mass riots, no curfew, no martial law declared, nothing. What's the world coming to? What's the Ayrshire Juniors coming to when bitter rivals like Auchinleck and Cumnock can meet up and just play football without war being declared in the region? Sad.

The game in Burns Country obviously needs an injection of new bad blood. Maybe someone could try to persuade Herfolge to pack in the Danish league and ground-share with, say, Beith or Maybole? Judging by the tactics the Danes employed against the 'Gers, they'd be well suited to the hurly-burly, rough-and-tumble, wacky world of the Ayrshire leagues of not-quite gentlemen. Did they like putting in the clog or what? They certainly left their Den-marks on a few shins, ankles and knees in the course of a particularly boring 90 minutes. However, not to worry. The important thing is Rangers coasted through and are now into the group stages of the Champions League.

'CRAIG BROWN'

See, the thing about being the Scotland boss: you've got to be nice to everybody, you've got to keep a cheery wee face on for the fans and never reveal the inner torment and self-loathing you feel when you've got to go on national television and say you'd take Duncan Ferguson back in a minute. But, errr, apart from Scotland, the squad and how the hell I'm going to forge a World Cup-qualifying team out of what's available, it's been quite an interesting weekend, hasn't it.

I was reading that Bert Konterman is a bit of an Eric Liddell. He's a deeply religious man who doesn't like playing football on a Sunday. Well, I see he stuck to his principles because he didn't play at all against Celtic. And what about Jim Jefferies having a go at Ivano Bonetti's Dundonian jersey-pullers. Seems to me 'Old Torn Face' should be grateful. If it hadn't been for jersey-pulling, then Hearts wouldn't have gotten themselves a penalty and would have ended up losing the game.

Of course, there's no way Juanjo overreacted when he was tugged. J.J wouldn't tolerate that in his team. I was also interested in the skills of Fab Caballero. On one occasion he was clean through but unfortunately, as *Scotsport*'s Peter Martin put it, 'He was put off by his left foot.' So, if only Fabbie had just the one foot then maybe he would have scored.

Incidentally, that's great news about Hamilton Accies being reunited with the B & Q Cup. Mind you, this does cause a massive headache for the builders currently constructing the Accies' new stadium. Now they'll have to build a trophy room.

THURSDAY, 31 AUGUST

So, the truth is out. The real reason Cristina Masetti – Big Amo's burd – went back to Italy is because she couldn't get enough modelling work in Scotland. Fair enough. Looking at Cristina you immediately think she just does not match up to the millions and millions of much better looking Scottish women competing in the lucrative world of Scottish modelling.

Apparently Big Lorenzo has been affected by his being chucked and it's been said it has been having an effect on his performances on the park. So far, the Italian Stale-Yin has blamed everyone and now his girlfriend for Rangers performance against Celtic . . . how about a wee swatch in the mirror, Amo?

Don't you just love watching the reaction amongst our soccer scribes when someone other than themselves criticises the state of Scottish football? It's as if only people living in Scotland – correction, make that only people living in Scotland who are paid for their opinions – are allowed to say bad things, slag off or basically just get ripped into the Scottish version of the beautiful game.

The latest rogue to transgress is Mark Viduka, who allegedly claimed that our game was so duff he only needed to play at 70 per cent of his capacity at Celtic and still managed to score a barrowload of goals and become Player of the Year. Granted, 70 per cent of Viduka's ability is more than 100 per cent of the majority of players currently plying their trade in Scotland. But for a man with a reputation for opening his gub and letting his billabong rumble, was this a gaff too far?

Of course, Viduka later denied ever having said anything like this, but haven't we heard this sort of thing before? Why, oh why are players always being misquoted? Even after strenuous denials will Viduka find that, if things aren't going too well for him, any crowd with a collective suspicious mind might think there is no smoke without fire and turn on this self-confessed lazy big so-and-so?

Anyway, be honest, say it is all 100 per cent – or even 70 per cent true – would we really be all that shocked? Smashing player, scorer of spectacular goals, great touch (for such a big man), strong as a kangaroo, aye, aye, aye. But to that list we might be inclined to add dim-witted too. When he didn't say the things he would never have said in the first place, it was probably just as well because all Viduka would have been doing was basically admitting he was a cheat. A cheat to the club who paid his wages and the supporters he claimed he loved. In the past there have been those who have suggested that Celtic fans don't support Scotland. Well, we reckon there might be a few will make a point of going along to Hampden for the upcoming Australia friendly just to say 'thank you' and 'cheerio' to Mark Viduka.

SEPTEMBER 2000

SATURDAY, 2 SEPTEMBER 2000

We've heard fans talk about signing players under the 'Bosnian ruling'. We've heard Manchester United being referred to as Manchester Un-tied. But perhaps the conversation one of us heard on Sunday morning sums up perfectly the state of play inside the head of your average football fan. 'I see Reggie Kray's been freed,' said one fan studying his newspapers. 'Who does he play for?' asked the other.

Spare a thought for Hibs boss Alex McLeish. That was a right double sickener he had to take last week, a real body blow to Hibs' chances this season. Didier Agathe decides to leave but, worse still, Gary Smith decides to *stay*.

SUNDAY, 3 SEPTEMBER

All together now:

> *Que sera, sera.*
> Whatever will be will be,
> we're going to Japan and Koree . . . a,
> *Que sera, sera.*

OK, make no mistake. A great result in Riga and arguably that's all that matters. But as for the match itself, well, what can you say? After the national anthems had been sung by what sounded like the Mormon Tabernacle Choir, we were subjected to 45 minutes with all the atmosphere of an edition of *Jeux Sans Frontieres* – Craig Brown having already played his joker, Matt Elliott at centre-forward.

ONLY AN EXCUSE?

The first half was dire. Craig had to do something and he did. He brought on Cameron and Naysmith (yes, that's how bad the Scotland squad is, you're looking to Hearts players to turn a match for you) – for the injured Weir and the rotten Davidson, moved Elliott back into defence and low and behold we improved from dire to woeful in one fell tactical swoop. Nippy Neil McCann grabbed us a late, late goal and suddenly commentators and summarisers stopped using words like 'industrious' and 'workman-like' and started using words like 'magnificent' and 'superb' instead. Just every now and again can't Scotland be involved in a right good football match like the Holland in orange and Ireland in green game which directly followed? This too, we bet, had a big audience in Scotland. Can you guess why? Holland, the country that gave us total football, were in a total shambles. It was the Irish crowd – most of them wearing the Hoops – who were making all the noise, giving it laldy to 'Da Fields of Athen-Roi' throughout the match.

It wasn't until Ireland were 2–0 up that the Dutch under Van Gaal – who must be a football genius because he makes lots of notes – started to play and managed to salvage a draw. Ronald de Boer? Mmm. Nice penalty-box dive in the first half to go with his attempt at a corner kick described by the commentator as 'the worst corner I've ever seen'. But then he did set up Holland's first goal with a lovely chip right on to Talan's head. It'll be interesting to see what this total footballer makes of the total madness of the Scottish game. There is, however, one question we have been pondering about the brothers de Boer. Which one do you think claims to be the good-looking one?

Dick Advocaat and John Hartson have something in common. Can you guess what it is? Is it:

(a) They are both Welsh,

(b) They are both Dutch,

(c) They have both had some sort of hair-restoring, miracle grass planted in their heads.

The answer is (c). Both men have had treatment to their nappers and in fact both men are proud to endorse it. That's why, no matter how depressed Hartson must have been over his proposed move to Ibrox falling through, he wouldn't be pulling his hair out. It's too expensive to replace.

OK, so the white bands under the ocksters will help camouflage unsightly sweat stains so you save on deodorant and – if you're really clatty – washing-up powder too. But the new, much-vaunted Scotland jersey is, well, pretty boring. Retro look? Classic? It's not that much different from so many other Scotland jerseys. I can see it being a big hit in the bars of Torremolinos but nothing for the aficionados to get excited about. Maybe that's the real reason Denis Law has been moaning about being used in the ad campaign. Not because he's not being paid but because the jerseys are mingin'.

MONDAY, 4 SEPTEMBER

So, Allan MacDonald has had enough. Now he just wants to get back to a nice, cosy 7.30 a.m. 'til 8.30 p.m. job outside football with only moderate amounts of stress and ulcer potential to deal with. Why? For the fact, alone, that he signed up Henrik Larsson on an improved deal, he could apply for and be granted the freedom of Celtic Park. So what made him hand in his notice? Was it the dream team fiasco? The Caley Thistle gubbing? Was

ONLY AN EXCUSE?

he just sick and tired of people coming up to him and asking, 'Hey, Allan, do *you* have any idea what Stephane Bonnes looks like?' No. We reckon he did it for the most noble of reasons. To save something that is very important to him – his waistline. Compare photographs of MacDonald when he arrived at Celtic Park and compare them to how he's looking today. Obviously the expense account lunches are taking their toll. Allan's wasting away to a mountain.

TUESDAY, 5 SEPTEMBER

Poor old Aberdeen. As if things weren't bad enough for the Dandy Dons, have they not had a £4,000 fine slapped on them because of their fans' behaviour in Dublin. What's not clear, however, is exactly just what their fans did. For a start I suppose them just turning up would have caused offence to a lot of people. Then, of course, much drink would have been taken, much merry banter would turn to much verbal abuse, the odd punch, the odd kick, the odd mass brawl. Of course, all this could have been avoided had the authorities just released a flock of sheep in O'Connell Street. There's nothing like a bit of romance to take the sting out of a situation.

'CHICK YOUNG'

Ho! Ho! Ho! Totally sensational! Superb! Magnificent! But enough about the nightlife in Riga, what about Scotland? With 89 minutes on the clock, I have to be honest and say I thought a draw was on the cards. But when Neil McCann – who's been sensational for Rangers this season, he really has, Advocaat has worked wonders with the wee man who has been a shining jewel in the glorious Rangers crown and ... er ... sorry – when Neil McCann cracked in that goal, I immediately predicted a victory for Scotland. I'll never forget the roar of shocked surprise in Rob MacLean's voice when the ball hit the onion bag, mainly because it woke me up from my sleep.

But, of course, the big story here in the land of the Lats was not the match itself but the alleged feud between the forces of purity and light and the forces of pure, evil badness. I am, of course, referring to the slight tension that may or may not have existed between the young Rangers superstar Barry Ferguson – Fergie, Bazza, Baz, The Great One, The Future King of Scottish Football – and that Gould of Celtic. Well, I can exclusively reveal that there was to be no square go behind the bike sheds. The pair were as friendly as two blokes who have nothing in common apart from their haircuts, and that has got to be great for Scottish football.

Of course, the icing on top of the cherry was when the Croatia/Belgium result came through, a pathetic 0–0 draw. Ya beauty! Without getting too carried away or anything, I think I can honestly say that, at that moment, we knew the Gods of Valhalla, Mount Olympus and Presbyteria were with us and that Scotland were going to qualify for the World Cup Finals, nae bother. Not even the news that England had drawn their friendly with France could upset the Tartan Army as they drank, displayed their really funny tee-shirts, did Highland flings and exposed their genitals to the locals. What characters. Makes you proud to be Scottish.

ONLY AN EXCUSE?

THURSDAY, 7 SEPTEMBER

You can't say Martin O'Neill hasn't tried with the Bhoy from Brazil but it's obvious it's just not working. There comes a time when you've just got to call a spade a spade and a Raphael a Scheidt and call it quits. That, in a sense, is what has happened. Brazilian club Corinthians have paid Celtic £300,000 – or was it the other way about? – to take Raph on loan with a view to a permanent move.

Ach well, we thought, good luck to him. He seemed a nice boy, a dud, but a nice boy. Then does he not go and get stuck into Celtic in particular and Scottish football generally as he heads back home. What a cheeky besom! 'Martin O'Neill,' says Raphael, 'told me to use my elbows more.' Well, when you can't hit the ball with your feet, you've got to try something. Then he had the damn cheek to say his time at Celtic Park was hell. Funny, but that's exactly the word used by everyone who ever saw him play.

We could be wrong but we reckon not even Celtic can cobble together a video about Raphael – but then again, let's wait and see. Mind you, questions still remain about his move back to Corinthians. Will he go back to central defence? Will he go back to being Scheidt? Probably.

SATURDAY, 9 SEPTEMBER

Overheard two friends talking, one from either side of the Old Firm. Commenting on the current League standings, Rangers fan says, quite sincerely, 'Aye, it'll be good if there's some competition this year.' The Celtic fan replies, 'Aye, I just hope Rangers can give us some.' Changed days, eh?

'Scottish football is rotten.' 'I only operated at 70%.' 'I'll score

20 goals for Leeds.' We had no sympathy at all when we heard the news that Mark Viduka had chipped a tooth in Leeds' home defeat at the hands of Man City, not because of the bad things the big Aussie has been saying about Scottish football but because it was probably self-inflicted. Every time Big Mark opens his mouth these days he puts his foot in it.

SUNDAY, 10 SEPTEMBER

By the way, we've just found out what it was the Aberdeen fans did in Dublin to warrant a hefty fine from UEFA. They were throwing coins. Aberdonians throwing away money? What's the world coming to?

MONDAY, 11 SEPTEMBER

The real joke about guys who sport a sweep-over hairstyle is that they honestly think they're getting away with it. They must think that everyone is looking at them and thinking, 'Oh look, there's so-and-so, he's not bald.' It's one of the great acts of self-delusion and Jim McLean has been party to such an act for years. Last week, however, all that changed. The most famous of the Brothers Grim shaved his head for charity. Well, that's not strictly speaking true, he didn't actually get his head shaved, he actually had about 30 extremely long strands of hair that were growing out the back of his neck cut. Having now got that technicality out the way we'd just like to say, well done to Jim McLean, it was a fine act. Although we just wonder, does the country need another dome?

'GRAEME SOUNESS'

Yeah for sure, you may have read about it in the newspapers, I've bought a new flat. It's got controlled entry, machine-gun towers, minefield and shark-infested moat but I wouldn't want fans to get the impression I'm aloof or anything. It's just that you never know when Chick Young might drop by. The reason I bought this flat is because Roy Keane, Denis Irwin and Teddy Sheringham are among some of the neighbours. I can't wait to get together for a game of football among the clothes poles, especially Roy Keane. God I'd love to go in for a 50/50 ball with Keane, just to see how tough he really IS – in a neighbourly way, of course.

Talking of Manchester United, I see Nike have offered Sir Alex Fergie an £8 million a year post when he quits management. Can I just remind Fergie of his good socialist principles and that Nike recently made the news for exploiting their workers by paying them a pittance in wages. So, I would urge Fergie to say no to Nike – then tell them I'd be interested.

Now, can I just say something here? Yeah for sure, things are going well at Blackburn. We're in fourth place, two points off the top. But you know me, I'm a winner, I won't be happy until we're at the top – or another club has come in and offered me a bigger salary to join them.

A lot of people keep asking me what's the latest over the proposed swap between Christian Daily and Eyal Berkovic. Well, I rate Eyal very highly. He's the kind of man who can win you a game – a game of Subbuteo, that is. Daily's form, on the other hand, is a bit inconsistent; he never quite turns it on all the time so, I suppose, he's not so much a Christian Daily as a Christian Monthly.

And what about that photo in the newspapers of Luc Nilis' leg breaking? Horrible, disgusting and yet you couldn't help but look at it. Exactly the same feeling when looking at a photo of Fabian Caballero's face.

Finally, will I be going to Coisty's new movie, *A Shot at Glory*, starring Robert Duvall, Ally McCoist, John Veigh and some of Coisty's pals? What do you think?

FRIDAY, 15 SEPTEMBER

Motagua. Some team, eh? What do you mean you've never heard of Motagua? The Motties? Only the best team in Honduras whose name begins with 'm'. Only the team whose star striker, Gustavo Fuentes – an Argentinian, so he must be good – definitely, maybe, possibly on his way to Dundee United. And that's not all. Francisco Ramirez and Reynaldo Clavasquin, two top-class, quality Honduran's, could be joining him.

Is this really the answer to Dundee United's problems? OK, if they do well and the fans are all singing and dancing, they'll be hailed as the Hon-Duran Durans. But you can't help thinking they just might struggle on Tayside.

We hear all three speak English with a touch of an accent. So what? In Dundee they speak accent with a touch of English. What if they don't like the climate? What if they don't like Jim McLean? What if they don't like 'Pehs', the staple diet of Dundonians? What if it's all a con? There are rumours that this is just a trick to appease the long-suffering Arab fans. That Wee Jim has bought a sunbed and is forcing youngsters to lie under it until they look suitably swarthy then they're being made to change their names to make them sound exciting.

Well, we hate to burst the bubble but we can exclusively reveal that we've heard that Gustavo Fuentes is actually Gus Ferguson from Kirkcaldy, Francisco Ramirez is Frank Ramsay from Milton and Reynaldo Clavasquin is Raymie Quin from Croy. And listen, these are quality rumours. We should know because we made them up ourselves.

ONLY AN EXCUSE?

SATURDAY, 16 SEPTEMBER

Why won't fans go and watch St Johnstone? They're a hard-working, very professional side and they play in a neat, if slightly Ibrox-looking, stadium. Their manager, Sandy Clark, is one of the most likeable guys in the game. They never draw any bad publicity – well, apart from George O'Boyle a few years back with a local barmaid, was it? They never do anything spectacularly good. They never do anything spectacularly bad. In fact, they just never do anything spectacular. You could say they are the living embodiment of unspectacular mediocrity. What must it be like watching a team like that week in, week out. Boring?

On Saturday's *Sportsound* Chick Young was taking pelters for suggesting, with tongue firmly in cheek – we think – that some of their players should attach themselves to the odd scandal to make the club sound interesting. Radical, but we can see where he's coming from. We disagree, though. If it's going to happen it's got to happen *on* the pitch. This is the team that, in the past, gave their fans the likes of your John Connollys and your Jim Pearsons. What have the scouts been doing? They need a right good kick in the Henry Halls.

Like every team, St Johnstone are calling out for an ageing, unfit, personality footballer to drain the club with his ridiculous salary demands but to pull in a few more curious punters along the way. And we know just the bloke. Diego Armando Maradona. What do you mean? Of course we're serious. If the wee man was playing at MacDermott Park would you not go and see him? Stick him in the middle alongside Paul Kane and they would scare the living daylights out of every other midfield in the country. Come on, would you want to go near those coupons if you didn't have to? OK, so Diego's maybe a few pounds overweight and deranged, but we were reading last week that he'd just smashed up his jeep so we reckon, throw in a new motor, and a deal could be done.

SUNDAY, 17 SEPTEMBER

Another book telling another 'real' story of Princess Diana is set to hit the shelves. Why are we not surprised? I suppose it's because it's what folk do, isn't it? Get a job with somebody famous, fall out with them, then cash in by betraying their trust and writing a book about them. It's cheap, it's low, it's despicable and it's what we both are secretly planning to do to each other in a few years time.

Where there's acrimony, there's a publishing deal so don't be surprised if, in the next few months, a Timography of tales appears surrounding the goings-on within Celtic Park in the past 12 months. Look out for *To Hell and Mac* by Allan MacDonald, *Barnes Stormer* by John Barnes, *Shut Up Your Gubs* by Kenny Dalglish, *Petta Late Than Never* by Bobby Petta, and *Honest This Is What Really Happened* by Michael Kelly. But if it's a good mystery you're after, then we recommend *A Brief History of Stephane Bonnes* by Dr Stephen Hawkings.

'TOMMY BURNS'

Errr, I think it would be very, very true to say that everyone at Celticfootballclub was very relieved and very, very happy with the result against Dunfermline on Monday night. We lost a bad goal, but then we bounced back and got a penalty of wur own – which was all the more sweet because Ian Ferguson gave it away. Was it a penalty? Well, Fergie phoned me up right away to assure me it wasn't. But as the Good Lord said in the Bible, 'Who gives a toss, we'll take it.' Then, up popped Henrik Larsson like an avenging angel to put to the sword Dunfermline's heresy. But I'm not getting carried away with things.

To be honest, in fact, to be very, very, very honest, I was very, very happy with the result. I would have been pure beelin' if we had dropped points, especially after giving the board such an easy time at the AGM. No questions about Raphael, about the NTL deal, about the duff screens at Celtic Park, about the debt, about Kenny Dalglish and the fact that he's suing Celticfootballclub. I think every shareholder present was so surprised to be getting into Celtic Park without having to cough up that they forgot why they were there.

Incidentally, Kenny suing the club isn't about money. It's about . . . er . . . it's about . . . errr . . . ach, it is about money. But something happened at Celtic Park on Monday that for me put everything into perspective. This was when they had to call for an anaesthetist to assist in Lubo Moravcik's haircut.

Finally, can I just say something very, very sincerely. I hope every true football supporter in Scotland will be behind Dick Advocaat's boys in the Champions League this week. This will be a tough game for the Hu . . . I mean Rangers. This isn't another Sturm Graz they're playing. Monaco will be a different kettle of fish, especially the big striker, a fish called Nonda.

FRIDAY, 22 SEPTEMBER

We wonder if David O'Leary received a mysterious phone call this week from someone with a voice that sounded suspiciously like Martin O'Neill's saying, 'I told you so.' And we wonder if he immediately knew the voice was referring to Mark Viduka?

So the big Aussie with such a delicate touch for a big man comes sauntering back two days late from that 'must-see' festival of football, The Olympic Games, without even as much as a note from his mammy saying, 'Please excuse Mark for being late for training, but he's a big self-centred so-and-so who just couldn't be arsed making the effort. Yours sincerley Mrs Viduka.' Like he really wanted to play for Australia in The Olympic Games. Like he really didn't want a wee break back home.

How did the Socceroos do? Did Viduka happen to score any goals? The whole thing smells like one of those MacDonald's Australian snacks Les Patterson has been advertising on the telly, gone bad.

For the record we just haven't been able to get into the Olympic football at all. The only incident that interested us was in the Brazil/Cameroon quarter-final when the two Brazilians were arguing and one ended up by nutting the other one. So much for Brazil being the home of 'the beautiful game'. But we reckon we're not alone. Folk who just associate football with the Olympics don't take it seriously and, anyway, there are too many other distractions like beach volleyball and watching the ladies' weight-lifting and sniggering like schoolboys every time the commentator says 'snatch'.

What England do under Kevin Keegan is entirely up to them, but surely the plan to make David Beckham captain should Tony Adams fail to make the opening match in their World

ONLY AN EXCUSE?

Cup-qualifying campaign is a bad move. The England captaincy was always given to guys like Billy Wright, Bobby Moore, Bobby Charlton. It was a job almost akin to that of Prime Minister. David Beckham whose kicks and tantrums and acts of petulance are legendary? Bad idea. See, that's where we, Scotland, are different from England. We would never go for someone like Beckham to captain us. We'd always go for an on-field diplomat of impeccable character and a temperate disposition. Someone like, say, Billy Bremner.

SATURDAY, 23 SEPTEMBER

We can't believe that Stewart Milne and the rest of the Aberdeen Board were duped by the internet hoaxer pretending to be bidding for the Dons' prize asset, Eoin Jess. Surely when they offered £545,000 for the player Milne must have cottoned on? I mean, £545,000 for Eoin Jess? Come on, nobody who knows anything about football is going to offer *that* much.

TUESDAY, 26 SEPTEMBER

See all this Old Firm breakaway nonsense? We reckon they should just forget it and stick with what they've got. The Champions League, that's the big one and we've got access to that, and our own domestic League is one of the most competitive in the world and for good solid reasons. If you are a Celtic supporter who would you rather see your team beat? Brondby, Boavista, Club Bruges or would you rather see them beat Hearts – (the Cousins of William), Kilmarnock, ('Hello, hello, we are the Killie Boys'), or Dunfermline ('Fergie's Volunteers')? While if you're a true blue do you really care if your team beat Roda, Standard Liege of Setubal more than if they beat Hibernian (the Tims from the East), Dundee United, (formerly Dundee Hibs and wearers of the green once more) or St Mirren (whom you've never forgiven for lying down to Celtic on the last day of the season in 1986 and depriving your Midlothian brothers of the Championship)?

The point being? The other league's grass is always greener. With us it's sectarianism, with other countries it's ethnic, political and sectarian too – we don't have a monopoly on it. Every team can come up with some non-football reason for hating the opposition. No real competition? Who's going to skoosh it this year? Matches have been tight, results are close. It's wide open. Only two in with any real chance? How many clubs have any real chance in every other country in Europe? Given we're just a wee ditty nation, two really big teams and a few below them looking to cause upsets is maybe as good as we can hope for. So OK, our League is rotten to its sectarian core. But hey, at least it's honest sectarianism.

'ALAN "RAMBO" McINALLY'

No … yeah … OK … seriously … I'm talking serious now … fitness has got nothing to do with it … trust me, fitness has got nothing to do with it. It's all about talent. That's why I'm reading a piece at the weekend, a good piece, a cracking piece, a right brammer of an article in the *Sunday Herald*, sister paper, I know, full of pundits who are great, great, good, good personal friends of mine and it was all about the Lazio goalie, my old Italian China from Italy, Angelo Peruzzi or Ango to his mates. Basically it was saying look at Peruzzi, he's a lardo but he's OK at football and it's true. I mean, not everyone can be, you know, well, like, how can I put it, an Adonis like me. But the thing is, why should they be? Get what I'm saying here? Course you do. Good. Well could you explain it to me?

See, like, yeah, uhhhmmm, OK, put it this way. When I was with Bayern in Munich with Bayern in Germany, there was a coach there, if you're of a certain, shall we say, age or a student of soccer like, shall we say, me, you might have heard of him, Gerd Müller, Wee Gerdie, Mullza – a great, great, good, good personal friend of mine and his name at the club was 'Dicker'. Know what that means in German? 'Fatty', 'fatso', 'tubby'. Even Franzie Beckenbauer, El Kaisero, he used to call Wee Mullza 'Dicker'. Did it matter to Gerdie? Not a bit, not a sausage. He was still arguably the second-best striker Bayern Munich ever had.

So, what's my point, caller? My point is that it doesn't matter if you're fat. You can still play football but you'll probably be rubbish and folk will laugh at you but hey, that's football.

But seriously, *seriously*, there are more serious things in life than football so what I'm saying is write to your MP now and demand he sort out the grim situation the country is facing on a weekly basis. Am I talking about the impending fuel crisis? No. I'm talking about wee Tommo McLean doing his side-kick to Arch on the Champions League.

THURSDAY, 28 SEPTEMBER

We hate to open old wounds but we just feel we have to comment on a recent auction of football memorabilia where an astonishing £92,000 was paid for the top worn by 'the man responsible for English football's finest hour' in the World Cup Final of 1966. We were slightly surprised to discover the top in question was the red one Geoff Hurst – sorry *Sir* Geoff Hurst – wore that day. If it was being billed as the top worn by the man responsible for England winning the World Cup, then surely it should have been the Russian linesman's jacket?

OCTOBER 2000

SUNDAY, 1 OCTOBER 2000

Mark Viduka: An Apology

Over the past few weeks we've been having a bit of a dig at the enigmatic Aussie with such a delicate touch for a big man. Well last week, against Besiktas, he answered this pair and all his other critics by getting it right up the lot of us in the best possible way. For Leeds against Besiktas he was sensational. OK, so he missed a good chance early on but he more than made up for it with a goal and what was it, three or four assists? Then on the Saturday he netted two in a minute against Spurs.

So, sorry, big man, we hold our hands up and say, sorry for ever suggesting you were a lazy, selfish, moody, self-centred, lying chancer who only turns it on when he takes it up his humph. We just don't know how we could ever have thought those things of you.

MONDAY, 2 OCTOBER

EXCLUSIVE!
Extract from Paulo di Canio's new book, *Football – The Beautiful Game . . . apart from Fergie, Brown and especially McCann*

Si. I Paulo. I show respect for the Rangers. Paulo have-a no problem with-a the Rangers. But Ian Fergie, bad man. He no like-a Celtic, he have-a no respect for Celtics or for Paulo so I try to show-a him how to respect, how to have passion, how to have love in his heart by threatening him to beat-a him to a pulp-a. And for some reason, he take offence at this. I no understand. You people in Scotland, you have-a strange attitude to people like-a me, people who like-a to take a right-a good maddie every once in a while.

Also I no like-a Fergus McCann, he is the devil, or Brown Jock, he is a demon from the bowels of hell or worse from the bowels of Scot FM. They break Paulo's heart because Paulo no want-a leave Celtic. It break-a Paulo's heart to have photo taken at-a Sheffield with big pizza and the stupid expression on-a my coupon. But-a maybe one day Paulo come back to Celtic, the club I love with all-a my heart, but-a only if the money is right, *capice*?

TUESDAY, 3 OCTOBER

Dominic Matteo. Because of his parentage, he can play for Italy or England, and because he was born in Dumfries he can also play for Jurassic Park. He's also played for England but now he's going to play for Scotland and be Scottish.

No, we don't understand it either. We always thought playing for your country meant, well, playing for your country not playing for your opportunity to show what you can do in the international shop window.

If you watched *Football Italia* on Sunday, you might have noted that Scotland boss Craig Brown was in Italy. Wonder if he was looking for any of Matteo's cousins to see if they wanted to play for Scotland?

'DAVY PROVAN'

Hello, reader, yes reader, well reader, what a week it's been for football, a quality week of sheer quality if ever there was one.

What about Celtic? After that result against Aberdeen I'm just wondering if now is the Winters of their discontent? They looked unsteady against the Dons, and it could have been worse if referee, Mike McCurry, had given that stonewall inconclusive penalty that Aberdeen should definitely have maybe been awarded. Once again it was down to Henrik Larsson to pull Celtic out of the mire. Which brings me to ask, do they need one more big-time player to give them another option? Could that option be Stan Collymore? There's a man who knows how to stamp his authority all over the opposition, especially if they're lying on the ground at the time. Collymore could be just the man to team up with two emerging hot-heads at Celtic Park, Bobby Petta – red-carded on Sunday – and Stilian Petrov – who's English is obviously improving if the arguments he now has with officials are anything to go by. In fact, inside Celtic Park they're known as The Pet Shock Boys.

But if I can just get back to Rangers, I have to say I'm all in favour of the new attitude that's sweeping throught he club. They seem to have rediscovered a sense of humour and realise that, OK, the punters want goals but they like a laugh too and Lorenzo Amoruso certainly gives them that with his free-kicks.

Can the Scottish Champions progress in Europe? When Rangers drew Monaco, Galatasaray and Sturm Graz everyone seemed to think they had a great chance of going forward into the second stages. They're in a good position but Galatasaray will be fired up for the return, Monaco will fancy themselves after finding a bit of form and Sturm Graz might just feel they can still sneak it. But if you were to push me then I'd have to say I'll go for Celtic.

ONLY AN EXCUSE?

WEDNESDAY, 4 OCTOBER

The pen may well be mightier than the sword but it could be that the court action is mightier than the pen. We'll soon find out as Fergus McCann announces he's having a legal square go with Paulo di Canio over comments made by the former Celt about the former 'Mr President' in his new book. At the end of the day, it's all going to come down to who the courts believe. Boring or what? Why doesn't Fergus write his own book giving *his* version of events and let the punters decide who they believe. We're sure it would be as big a seller as Jock Brown's *Celtic Minded*. Then again, maybe there's another reason for taking the litigious route. Could, after all these months of obscurity, Wee Fergus be missing the limelight? When he was 'Mr Celtic' you got the impression that, like some Wild West gunfighter, the McCann with No Name thrived on the notoriety he had for being a straight-talking, pugnacious *hombre* who liked a good scrap. Maybe he's discovered that, for all the cash in the bank, pushing the baby buggy around some millionaire's playground in big Bermuda shorts just doesn't match up to the cut and thrust of Scottish football.

At the end of the day all this court action means is that a few more people will buy Di Canio's book because of the publicity McCann's action will generate. It's so predictable you could even be forgiven for thinking that that's the whole idea in the first place.

FRIDAY, 6 OCTOBER

Back in 1990, when Claudio Caniggia ran through to score the goal that knocked Brazil out the World Cup, we turned to each other and said, 'One day that boy will play for Dundee.' Honest, we did. There was just something about him. Ten years later there's still something about him. Maybe it's the Francis Rossi of Status Quo – circa 1974 – hairstyle. Maybe it's the glamorous, model-burd wife. Maybe it's the 'Red Hand of Argentina' tattoo just at the bottom of his thumb. But 33-year-old Claudio still looks the part – the part being Jennifer Aniston in *Friends*.

Another thing that gives Claudio an aura is the fact that he doesn't speak English. Funny how when it's a foreign chappie standing there who can't speak our language, it gives them a sort of mystique but when it's a Scotsman who can't speak a foreign language, they just look stupid.

To be absolutely honest, there's something just completely mad about this whole situation. Nothing against Dundee. After all, we've now become used to having the club associated with glamorous names like Nemsadze, Caballero and Tweed. But at a reported £15,000 a week this all sounds like a very expensive short-term fix. Sorry, Claudio, no pun intended.

One spin-off, though. Could mean a massive boost to the local economy. Diego Maradona has promised to come to Dens Park to see his old pal Caniggia play. 'Peh' makers get ready for a windfall.

'SIR ALEX FERGUSON'

Proud. Oh yes. Very proud of the way my players played for their respective countries last weekend. Very Proud. And very proud of what we raised in a charity match at the weekend and very, very proud of myself for managing to wear a Celtic top in that charity match and not getting the dry boke once.

But, of course, the big story of the week isn't the fact that I, Sir Fergie, wore the hoops. No, the big talking point isn't so much a talking point as a question, and that question is this. Kevin Keegan, is he an honourable man or is he just a snivelling, lily-livered, wee bottler who runs a mile at the first sign of a problem? Well, to be perfectly honest, I really wouldn't like to say.

I'm not saying Kevin is a bad manager or anything like it, but with all the players he has you'd think he could do something at international level. In central defence, Keown and Adams – they're frightening, scary even, look like a couple of extras from *Night of the Living Dead*. In goal, well, what can you say about David Seaman other than what's a man his age doing with a stupid hairstyle like that? As for Michael Owen? I feel that the strain of being labelled the 'English Mark Burchill' has taken its toll. I suppose, what I'm saying is, I blame the players. I do. I blame the players. Every single one of them … apart from maybe Beckham and Cole … and possibly Scholes and the Neville brothers and Sheringham and every other Manchester United player past, present or future that has or will play for England. I can't be any more fair-minded than that.

MONDAY, 9 OCTOBER

Ach, well, I suppose we better say something about Scotland and San Marino. Now be honest, as the match reached half-time didn't you think about all the gloating you'd been doing over England's result and wonder if we were going to be paid back for our smugness? How bad were Scotland? Well, you know how, as is traditional after a big match, the newspapers give the players marks out of ten? Well, in some papers, if you took each individual player's marks and added them all together then you might just about have made a mark of ten for the entire team. Now, of course, an even weaker side than the weakened side that played Croatia has now got to play the stronger side Croatia. We do have this sneaking suspicion that Scotland could possibly lose this one.

WEDNESDAY, 11 OCTOBER

Regular viewers of BBC's *Weekend Watchdog* won't be surprised to hear that an old boot came in for severe criticism last week and this time, for once, it wasn't Anne Robinson. The boot in question was the Adidas Predator, the top-of-the-range model, as endorsed by David Beckham, that'll set you back around £120 a pair. The problem? The blades – the things that have replaced studs – are shoogly, making it very difficult to run without falling over.

Anyway, we're sure, whatever the problem is, the brainy folk at Adidas will figure out what it is and fix it. But it doesn't alter the fact that, as football boots go, Predators are hellish looking. Why have boot designers abandoned the classic lines of the past like Continentals, with their re-enforced steel toecaps? Or Goal

ONLY AN EXCUSE?

Speedsters, a football boot based on the classic design of the wooden clogs worn by Dutch people in the last century? Screw in studs? What was wrong with nails? Kids today. They don't know what they're missing.

THURSDAY, 12 OCTOBER

Greater love hath no man than to give up his super-model burd for the game.

That's what Manchester United's Fabien Barthez has had to do after Linda Evangellista announced last week she, rather surprisingly we thought, still prefers the French Riviera to Manchester and has legged it back to Monaco. Of course, the big question in all this isn't, 'Why did Barthez think Manchester could rival the French Riviera?' It's 'How did Barthez manage to pull a super-model burd in the first place?' There's obviously something about a smooth pate that attracts the female ladies of the opposite sex. Or, to put it in layman's terms, for some inexplicable reason baldies pull burds, or, to be more precise, baldies in football pull burds. Why is this? We don't know. All we can do is exclusively reveal that, in his own country, Barthez is known as 'Le Chick'. We can't for the life of us think why.

SATURDAY, 14 OCTOBER

We both knew something was seriously wrong when Dougie Vipond introduced *Sportscene Match of the Day* and the customary welcoming smile on the presenter's face was conspicuous by its absence. In fact, so serious was Dougie's dish that we thought war had been declared. Well, in a sense I suppose it had. Rumours were rife of an incident at Tannadice after Radio

Clyde's Mark Hateley broke off from the Phone-in to give a blow-by-blow account that Harry Carpenter would have been proud of. Now we were going to get the BBC version.

When Dougie mentioned the word 'unedited' then we knew we were in for a treat, and we were. Drama? This was better than *Casualty*. If anyone ever wondered why Dundee United were known as 'The Terrors' they were about to find out. Now, we know it's hard to tell when Jim Mclean is in a bad mood and when he isn't, but we feel the quavering voice and the unblinking eyes fixed on John Barnes' face like laser sights were a bit of a giveaway.

Then Barnes – soon to become the Kate Adie of Scottish sports broadcasting – asked a question about Jim's wee brother, Tommy, coming back to the club. The cage was definitely rattling and when he followed this up with an inquiry about Alex Smith's future . . . *BINGO*! McLean snaps and allegedly punches John Barnes, who was then seen to have red stuff, allegedly blood, pouring allegedly from a nose that was allegedly attached to his face.

Within minutes the Dundee United Board had acted quickly and informed Jim he had been 'resigned'. As word of the incident spread, the crowds protesting outside Tannadice quickly legged it just in case Wee Jim came out and got tore into them as well. Whatever you thought of 'the Wee Joiner', whatever you think of what he did last Saturday, it's worth remembering that he did win the League. Who can ever forget that day back in 1983 when his team won and there was Jim, walking along the touchline, arguing with cameramen, fans and basically anybody who approached him with too big a smile on their face. Even in his finest moment, all he could do was moan.

Next week, we were just wondering, will there be a minute's

silence at all Scottish football grounds to mark the passing of the career of Jim McLean?

SUNDAY, 15 OCTOBER

Did you ever think you'd see the day when Scotland would go to Croatia, come away with a 1–1 draw and you'd be disappointed? Don't know about you but that's how we felt on Wednesday night. If big Colin Hendry's forehead just wasn't so flat, or Don Hutchison had only managed to miss-kick that shot a wee bit better then the game was ours, no question about it. And yet it started so badly for us. See when Alen Boksic nicked in behind Matt Elliott, controlled the ball perfectly with one foot then buried it with the other, we both thought, 'Aw naw, we are gonnae get so gubbed.' Even when Colin 'Mad Dog' Cameron battled on gamely to provide the cross which led to Kevin 'the Hit Man' Gallacher nabbing the equaliser, we put this down to Croatia switching off momentarily and being caught out, fully expecting them to come roaring back and severely molicating us. And yet, strangely, at the end of the game, we were left thinking, 'We coulda won that.'

This was a fighting performance to be proud of.

One thing we'd like to draw attention to, though. We just felt that the backroom boys on the bench could have done so much more. Coming back after half-time, Archie Knox walked straight past two Croatian subs and didn't even attempt to have a kick at them.

'KENNY DALGLISH'

There's no maybes aye or maybes no about it, I had a job to do at Celtic Park and I was doing it. So was John Barnes, Eric Black and Terry McDermott. They were all doing my job too and I was doing theirs. In fact, we were all doing each other's jobs and maybe that was the problem. So we brought in Tommy Burns and told him to do our jobs as well and he did, but that's football. Sometimes, at the end of the day, you've just got to hold your hands up or even your hands out and say, OK, things isnae working out the way you would have liked, but that's football as well.

Some people think that success will come to you on a plate, some think that it will come to you wrapped up in a newspaper. All I can say is I hope it comes to me in a brown envelope.

At the moment, though, you would have to say that things is looking no' bad for Celtie. Maybe no' as no' badder as we would have made them if we'd still been there, but the bookies have installed Celtic as favourites to win the league and I promise the fans that when I do get my settlement from the club, I'll be putting at least a tenner on them.

I seen that Didier Agathe made a successful début, but he never cost anything so what's good about that? What would the fans rather see at Celtic Park? El cheapos who are good players or vastly overrated expensive flops who kiss the jersey?

Most interesting development of all, though, has to be the news that a player from another Scottish club at the centre of an Old Firm tug-of-war – Robert, Rab or Bobby Douglas, depending on what newspaper you read – has chosen to come to Celtic as opposed to Rangers. Previous tug-of-war stars, Gordan Petric and Darius Adamczuk, chose Rangers and look how it worked out for them. I'm sure all the Rangers fans will be wishing the same good fortune to Big Robert or Rab or Bobby.

ONLY AN EXCUSE?

THURSDAY, 19 OCTOBER

There was one piece of news recently that, we have to say, took us by no surprise at all. The shock announcement that Duncan Ferguson is out for the rest of the year thanks to a new kick on an old injury. It's a pretty unique achievement all the same – your comeback game and your swansong both on the same day.

The Bird Man Fae Bannockburn might have all the extras, but on top of the classy chassis he's still a bit of a Lada Riva. He's got everything you'd want in a footballer apart from 24-hour breakdown cover. We're afraid Big Dunc is just living proof of the old adage: 'Those who can, do. Those who can't, keep doos.'

SATURDAY, 21 OCTOBER

We can't confirm that this is 100 per cent true but a friend of ours who sells the *Evening Times* outside the Vatican claims that, when the Queen met the Pope last week, the first thing Her Majesty said to the Pontiff was, 'So, J.P., I see that your Tims benefited from more dodgy refereeing decisions at St Johnstone.' To which the Pope allegedly replied, 'Aye, an' what about it?' Our newspaper-vending friend then went on to tell us that the Pope then exclusively revealed to HRH that the Third Secret of Fatima is that Celtic will win the Championship this season.

We have to say, all the signs point to a year of triumph for the 'Tic. We don't know if you've noticed but there are, in fact, a whole load of coincidences between this season and 1988 which point to Celtic ending the season on top:

- Billy McNeill was the new boss at Celtic in 1988; Martin O'Neill is the new boss at Celtic in 2000.

- McNeill and O'Neill are very similar names.
- Even spookier, Billy McNeill has a son called Martin.
- Now, if these facts haven't convinced you Celtic will win the League then read on:
- Celtic wore hoops in 1988; they're wearing hoops in 2000.
- In 1988 the grass at Celtic Park was green; in 2000 the grass at Celtic Park is green.
- In 1988 Frank MacAvennie was making headlines; in 2000 Frank MacAvennie is making headlines.

Of course, maybe the most crucial factor of all is the one already touched on by the Queen – the fact that, this season, the Hoops have had a fair share of crucial refereeing decisions go their way. The penalty given against Dunfermline; the free-kick retaken against St Johnstone: the penalty awarded in the same game: the penalty *not* given to Aberdeen; and Tommy Boyd *not* being sent off for his involvement in this incident. You know, we wouldn't be surprised if Rangers fans took a long hard look at this and claimed that some Knights of Saint Columba plot was being hatched. As for the Celtic fans, the question needing to be asked is, will this run of fair play – or, dare we say it, favouritism – finally allay all fears of conspiracy and dispel all paranoid notions of Masonic misappropriations and Proddie subterfuge? Don't be ridiculous.

A lovely touch that, having kids in Hearts strips coming out with the Hibs team and *vice versa*. All the same, we couldn't help but feel sorry for the wean that got Steve Fulton. We can only hope they don't have too many nightmares. Incidentally, you really can only marvel at the size of 'The Player Formerly Known as Baggio's arse'. Where does he get his shorts, do you think? Mr High and Mighty?

ONLY AN EXCUSE?

Anyway, as we watched this game there were only two questions that kept rattling around inside our heads. How does six-foot-seven Kevin James manage to seem smaller when he jumps for the ball. And would Davy Provan pick Henrik Larsson as his Man of the Match?

MONDAY, 23 OCTOBER

Bordeaux versus Celtic? Well, the Celtic defence are going to have to really be on their toes. Goals for Bordeaux could come from any number of players: Sonny Anderson, Christophe Dugarry, Paul Lambert – who incidentally is now Dundee United's second-top scorer. In the end, though, we feel it's all going to come down to pace. They might just be a wee bit faster up front than what the Hoops are used to facing. So, for their Sonny Anderson Celtic have to find a Sonny Corleone and for their Dugarry a Dirty Harry. In other words, they might have to be a bit physical – just to put these nippy, continental types off their stride, you understand.

'STEWART MILNE'

Aye, well, fit like, things has been pretty tough at Aiberdeen lately. It's been like the Alamo up here. Some folk say that's why I walk about with a Davy Crockett hat on my head. But all that's changing now with the arrival of the new chief executive, David 'Dave' Cormack. He's already set to work and hopes to come up with answers to questions that have had us stumped for years like, 'What does Keith Burkinshaw actually do?'

On the transfer front we've been looking at big stars like Billy McKinlay and Willie Falconer so, as you can see, we're looking to the future.

We're also really pleased about the news regarding Eoin Jess. We offered him more money than we've ever offered anyone before, plus a testimonial plus Gordon Bennett's wee black book and, guess what, he's decided to accept our offer and go away. I heard a rumour that Bryan Robson's Middlesbrough might be interested in Eoin, although as their signing policy seems to be only to buy fading has-beens I don't know if they'd be interested in a rising never-was.

I'm also really pleased to see that Ebbe is now sporting a more mental, sticky-up hairstyle. To me it makes him look much tougher, without losing his human touch. A sort of cross between Kirk Douglas in *Spartacus* and Limahl in Kajagoogoo.

So, all in all, things is looking up at Aiberdeen. We've got our ambition back and we just can't wait to get right back up there to the very middle of the table where we belong.

WEDNESDAY, 25 OCTOBER

No offence to our Austrian readers but Sturm Graz have got to be one of the worst teams we've ever seen playing in the Champions Leagues. And yet, there they are in a good position to qualify for the second stages of the competition after winning their third home game without losing a goal.

The Teddies took a fair dose of pelters from certain sections of the media for their totally inept performance, but it's actually quite hard to gauge just how bad Rangers were, given how bad Sturm Graz were too. What the Austrians did have, though, was confidence bordering on arrogance. They even showed contempt for Rangers by substituting their best player – a blatant case of extracting the Yuran if ever their was one. Overall, though, we just thought they were Fleurquin rotten.

But what about the 'Gers? Let's analyse the performance. Wee Dick's tactical masterstroke this time, three at the back – or, given that one of the three was Amoruso, two at the back – didn't work. Ball-watching, uncertainty, lack of confidence, lack of pace, lapses of concentration – you name it, the 'Gers defence were at it. We thought 'The Kaiser' would step into the breech, but he was too busy trying to look busy in midfield, while Y-Bazza moaned and winced and grimaced his way through a largely frustrating 90 minutes. Up front you had wide-boy Kanchelskis, who was so bad he didn't even get into a position to make one of his legendary dives. Rod Wallace, obviously not fit, and R. de Boer, obviously there to pull the strings – which is a fitting job for someone who looks like a Gerry Anderson puppet.

A wee word about the goalie? Oh, why not. The £2 million Jesper Christiansen? They would have been better off signing

Liz Christiansen – wee joke for the old folks there. J.C. was no saviour on the night. Looking more like a singer out of a boy band, he's just too good looking to be a goalie. Handsome keepers? Bad idea. They don't want to risk their looks.

Now, this might sound a wee bit radical, but see in the future, whenever Rangers get a free kick, one of their players has got to take the ball away from Amoruso and just tell him, 'Naw, Amo, you're no' taking the free kicks and that's final.' Or, alternatively, get four or five players to hold him down until after the kick is taken. The captain's free kicks are so bad they evoke memories of the old John Greig tactic of kicking the ball out the stadium to waste time. Now, to be fair to Amo, the last free kick he took in Graz was only, what, two maybe three yards over the cross-bar? Another four or five goes and he might have been hitting the target.

If, however, there was a clever piece of Advocaat strategy on the night, then could it have been the substitution that saw Marco 'Moody Blue' Negri take to the field? All those fans on all those phone-ins wanting to see Negri getting a game? Well, Advocaat gave them what they wanted. Be honest, apart from when he ran on to the pitch, was Negri's name mentioned again? We wonder, Was this the manager's way of shutting up the 'Why doesn't Advocaat play Negri?' brigade once and for all?

Finally, what about poor old Arthur Numan? Appropriately enough for a match being played in the Arnold Schwartzenegger stadium some of the tackling was straight out of *Conan the Barbarian*. And yet the only guy to be sent off is Numan for two yellow cards picked up for coming back on to the pitch without permission – allegedly – and obstruction. No wonder he was beelin'! But did he really need to remove his shirt and display his torso? Surely there were enough tits on view already?

ONLY AN EXCUSE?

THURSDAY, 26 OCTOBER

If you use as your yardstick Celtic's previous performance against a French club in the UEFA Cup just 12 months ago then you would have to say, yes, they have most certainly improved. True, Celtic must have received a huge psychological boost when they saw the referee and he looked like John Rowbotham but it's the confidence O'Neill has instilled in the team that is most impressive. Jonny Gould has the confidence to judge when the ball is going to hit the post so he doesn't need to bother going for it, and what about Bobby Petta? Confident enough to go crashing to the ground every time an opposition player so much as brushes against him.

Despite having the word 'Siemens' emblazoned across the front of their tops, Bordeaux lacked spunk. Not until towards the end, when some of their more petulant stars started taking the cream puff and getting a bit more physical, did they justify their Airdrie-style jerseys.

But Celtic fans take note, it's only half-time. This tie isn't over yet and don't forget there are some excellent players in this team. The pace of Pauleta, the class of Dugarry and what about Laslandes and his superb control? See the way he trapped Henrik Larsson's head.

FRIDAY, 27 OCTOBER

Allegations of violence and intimidation have been sneaking out of the Procurator Fiscal's office in Dundee where charges were sensationally dropped against Jim 'Mad Dog' McLean. Apparently the Procurator – or is it the Fiscal? – asked Jim McLean, 'Did you strike the reporter John Barnes?', to which

Mr McLean answered, 'Do you think I'm going to answer a stupid question like that?' then various thumps and sweary words were heard and, *voila!*, the case was dropped.

In the meantime, what about the innocent victim in all of this, John Barnes? Word is he's taking the road to not so bonnie Dundee for a legal 'square go' and he's looking for hauners. Word is he's even considering phoning up lunchtime *Scotland Today* and asking Austin Lafferty – the Chick Young of the legal profession – for his advice. Now that's serious. All in all, though, we can't help but wonder if, deep down, Barnesy just wishes he'd belted Wee Jim back and avoided all this legal mumbo-jumbo.

SUNDAY, 29 OCTOBER

Their number one goalie is in a treatment room somewhere having a Klos Encounter of the Physio kind; Charbonnier is playing the Scarlet Pimpernel somewhere in France; and Big Rab Douglas, who sounds like and looks like a Rangers goalie, chose Celtic Park over Castle Greyskull. They have had terrible luck on the transfer front. They didn't get Hartson, they didn't get Tamudo, they *did* get de Boer. A product of the Ajax School of Excellence, Ronnie has certainly showed his versatility since arriving at Ibrox. He's been rotten in a number of positions.

Now there's a thought. Have the Teddy Bears now officially changed their name to 'Injury Ravaged Rangers FC'? The footie press, slow at first, are gradually coming round to the idea that, due to recent results, form and League position, it's now actually valid to have a wee snipe at the 'Gers. However, we still get this feeling that an all-out, concerted attack is being held back because what if Rangers do turn things round and all those who criticise end up on Wee Dick's black list? How could they survive? And what are Rangers doing all this time?

Expect the Ibrox PR department – or, as you know it better, *Friday Night Sportscene* – to launch a major offensive. An 'exclusive' interview with David Murray is surely imminent.

'DENIS LAW'

Well, you know, as I say, you've got to hand it to Alex McLeish, right? You really have. He's doing really well for himself, so he is. His team, Hibs of Hibernian, are up there in second place *and* he's just landed the job of First Minister. Well done, Alex. And young Bobby Williamson at Killiemarnock? Somebody said to me the other day, 'Denis,' they said, because – coincidentally – that is my name, 'Denis, some result the Killiemarnock got at Ibrox, 3–0.' I said to them, '3–0 at Ibrox, who were they playing?'

But, hey, what about Celtic? Martin O'Neill's doing a tremendous job there and I hear the FA are interested in him as the new England boss because, let me tell you, boy, England are struggling and O'Neill would be good for them because if there's one thing the English need, it's the luck of the Irish.

And talking of the Irish, what about Di Canio, eh? His agent has been offering him back to Celtic. Would that be a bad move or merely a disaster? I mean, don't get me wrong. He's a fabulous player. But he's also got an Italian temperament. Now that could have something to do with him being Italian. I do know about these things because I did actually once play for Turino, one of Italy's top Italian clubs. But the thing is, right, nutter or not he could also play a bit too, and maybe or even possibly Martin O'Neill would be willing to take a chance with his nuttery because, after all, he was willing to take a chance with Stanley Collymore who I see was in trouble for his celebrations after scoring against Leeds on Sunday. Stupid boy. I mean, when you're basically saying, 'Get it right up you' to the opposition fans, you've got to apply a little subtlety – like the way Eric Cantona used to do it with a kung fu kick. Now that's what you call class.

NOVEMBER 2000

THURSDAY, 2 NOVEMBER 2000

The CIS Cup. Not that we feel no one takes this competition really seriously any more but the quarter-finals in November, the semi-finals in February? When are they going to play the final? The day before or the day after the Scottish Cup Final?

We have to say we were not in the least surprised with the draw. They usually contrive to keep the two good teams apart, and that's exactly what they did. Celtic and Kilmarnock managed to avoid each other. But we wouldn't rule out a shock. Don't write off a Rangers/St Mirren final just yet.

SATURDAY, 4 NOVEMBER

The draw for the CIS Cup semi-finals took place and it has been stated that no representatives from Rangers were present. This, we can exclusively reveal, is simply not true. Chick Young was definitely present.

Leaving aside the fact that St Mirren had eight players out injured – remember, Rangers are the only team in Scotland who ever have injuries – does the 'Gers' 7–1 thrashing of the beleaguered Buddies mean that the Rangers crisis is over and they are simply the best again? We reckon there are a lot of relieved scribes out there who were so obviously uncomfortable at having to go against their instincts and criticise the men from Castle Greyskull. On both radio stations we switched between on Saturday, the sense of relief was almost palpable.

Now, of course, everyone is entitled to support whoever they want to support, but whatever has happened to surely that pre-requisite of sports journalism, objectivity? Interviews – exclusive or otherwise – should surely sound like interviews and not like wee boys gasping at everything their hero says. After listening to and studying radio broadcasts for the past 15 years we have come up with the *Only An Excuse?* theory of subjectivity. Celtic-supporting meedja-types, no matter how good they are at their jobs, are always that wee bit more critical of Celtic. Rangers-supporting meedja-types, no matter how good they are at their jobs, are always that wee bit more praising of Rangers. Why not put it to the Radio Clyde test and see if we're right?

SUNDAY, 5 NOVEMBER

If you don't lose any goals then you can't be beaten. Mind you, if you don't score any goals then you can't win. But surely, if you're losing all the time then before you think about winning games again, you should first try drawing some. Makes sense? Of course it does. So, it's therefore easy to see the logic in Dundee United's latest signing, someone who can shore up the entire midfield by himself, Charlie Miller. Did you see the size of him? At least free kicks will no longer be difficult for United to defend. Charlie can be the wall all by himself.

'Money, money, money, must be funny, in a rich man's world.' They Abbas certainly knew what they were talking about. But hold on. Before the rest of the footballing world faints at the size of the new deal between Manchester 'Richest Team in the Country' United and Nike – a cool £302.9 million – just remember. It is over 13 years so it's not really as massive as it sounds. When you break it all down, it's only a mere

£23.3 million a year, so nothing to get too worried about, OK?

MONDAY, 6 NOVEMBER

There are probably a lot of embittered Celtic fans out there who were hoping and praying that Mark Viduka would fall flat on his arse when he moved to Leeds. Well, that just hasn't happened. The big Ozzie is on fire, and that's got to be a good thing – if only because it gets it right up Mark Lawrenson who's never done slagging off the Scottish game. OK, so Viduka might have been offside for his fourth goal on Saturday, but only about 70 per cent offside, surely?

'CRAIG BROWN'

Errr, weeelll, yes, I would have to say, I am still hurting just a wee bit over the things James Leighton accused me of in his scurrilous book. For the cheeky besom to say that I asked him to fake an injury is nothing short of sheer impishness. I can assure you I've never had anyone under me ever fake anything.

I see young Charles Miller is back home in Scotland and I hear Alexander Smith is saying he should get a cap, and I agree with that. Charles *should* get a cap – a nice woolly one to keep that big head of his warm after his move from the tropics, Watford, to the frozen wastelands of Dundee.

Just before I go, can I just say a word about England appointing a foreign coach, Steven Goran Erickson? I sincerely hope that we don't go down that road. I mean, what would the game be coming to if, in the future, we started trusting our national side to someone who knows what they are talking about. Mind you, Erickson's Swedish, isn't he? Wonder what his wife looks like?

TUESDAY, 7 NOVEMBER

Does Eyal Berkovic have his own website? If he doesn't then maybe he should think about creating one. Websites seem to be the 'must-have' toy for footballers these days especially footballers with a habit of mouthing off. After having his lawyer send a letter to his boss, Martin O'Neill, demanding that Eyal get a game we thought, what next, a note from his mum? But no, the Israeli international opted for the tried and trusted route, a right good whinge to the press.

It's a 'nightmare' says Eyal, a man on 28 grand a week. 'I was told I would be getting a game,' says Eyal, a man who made a 'get it up you' gesture the last time he scored. 'I want to get back to playing with Souness again,' says Eyal. Did no one bother to tell the wee man not to mention the 's' word? To many Celtic supporters that name is up there with other designations like Beelzebub, Lucifer and Satan.

WEDNESDAY, 8 NOVEMBER

At the start of the season, Rangers were so good they had two teams that, according to the press, were both capable of winning the Championship. Now the talk is of Rangers paying off a load of their players to just go away and not come back. That £2 million UEFA money David Murray has promised Dick Advocaat could be used up getting old players *out* the door rather than bringing new ones *in*. When you look at the amount of money Advocaat has spent in the past 18 months – and not forgetting the follicular connection – then it's easy to see why the Ibrox boss is fast becoming the Elton John of Scottish football.

Rangers are struggling, Celtic are flying and this weekend comes the second Old Firm match of the season. Judgement Day, The Day of Reckoning, The Day of the Triffids, Day-oh, dayyy-oh, daylight come and I wanna go home. Call it what you like but one thing's for sure. It's going to be what Jock Wallace would have described as a match for 'fixed bayonets'. Don't be fooled by the pundits. The form book *does* matter in an Old Firm match but only for about the first two minutes. Then it's all down to which team wants to win it more, which team is more up for it on the day or which team goes the mentalest on the day.

Predictions? Well, if Rangers win then we predict Advocaat will once again be hailed as 'The Little General', master tactician and manager extraordinaire. If Celtic win then the League race will be over until the next time they drop any points when it will be back on again. But we reckon, no one's going to win. We reckon tension will be too high for good football, nerves will play too big a part and we reckon you're looking at a dull, low-scoring draw. Say maybe 4–4?

THURSDAY, 9 NOVEMBER

Death was the big television box-office draw last Wednesday. You had Inspector Morse dying on ITV and Scotland dying on the pitch at Hampden. We know it was only a friendly, but this was brutal. Scotland were rotten. Maybe it's just as well Mark Viduka wasn't playing, we might have taken a right gubbing.

Match highlights on the pitch? Errr . . . pass. Match highlights *off* the pitch? Difficult to choose between the antics of the stewards confiscating an inflatable crocodile from some fans, the police telling a bunch of weans, 'There will be no congo lines here', and the inevitable 'Whenever there's a boring match at Hampden' streaker.

If there's anything good to come out of this débâcle, it's Craig Brown's announcement that that's him finished with friendlies. Great idea. Maybe it was the pressure of being the country rated 20th in the world playing the country rated 74th. Maybe it was the rain. Maybe it was because most of the squad wanted to be at home watching *Morse* on the telly. Anyway, we're sure Craig Brown did get a huge lift later on in the week when his beloved brother, Jock, was axed from his Scot FM *Drive Time* radio show. Apparently the former Celtic whatever it is he was, was receiving barely seven calls per hour. I don't know about you but when we heard that, we were shocked. Seven calls? That many?

FRIDAY, 10 NOVEMBER

I don't think anyone was really surprised when it was announced that Jim Jefferies was to be the new boss of Bradford City. The reasons cited for him being a good appointment for the Bantams is that he's good at bringing through youngsters and at working miracles with small amounts of money. True, when he was with The Jambos he constantly brought through excellent youngsters. But working miracles with small amounts of money? Bringing in mediocrities and paying them more than your club can afford is hardly shrewdness. Bradford City are currently bottom of a very tough League, and J.J. doesn't really have the luxury of a few years to develop some youngsters so he'll have to buy. Presumably Jim has been promised a few bob to spend, so will he be cautious and canny or will he be like a wean in a sweetie shop and go daft? It'll be interesting to see if the Hearts supporters still have a great affection for their former boss if he suddenly turns round, ram raids Tynecastle and makes off with their best players.

ONLY AN EXCUSE?

We don't know if we'd describe Jim as a scrapper, but he's certainly a moaner so we look forward to seeing how the likes of Sir Fergie, Arsene, O'Leary and other managerial giants of the English game react to J.J. constantly claiming his team dominated the match and were unlucky to lose.

SUNDAY, 12 NOVEMBER

Both having had previous engagements – see that Michael Douglas and Catherine Zeta Jones, do they know how to put on a purvey, or what? – neither of us were able to attend the Challenge Cup Final at Broadwood. Given the rotten time Airdrie has been having recently – even the town itself has just picked up some sort of Midden of the Year award – it was good to see The Onians, The Diamonds, The In-Laws of William, give the locals a lift by winning the trophy. Well done, Archie and *los hombres Airdrieosos*. To be honest, we fancied Livingston to do the business. with a Crabbe in their side we thought they'd be itching for success.

'WALTER SMITH' and 'TOMMY BURNS'

TOMMY: Errr, Walter, I am very, very pleased to see you.

WALTER: Obviously, particularly, at the present moment, nice to see you too.

TOMMY: I suppose the reason we have been brought together here is to discuss wur experiences in the build-up to an Old Firm match.

WALTER: Let's see, what do I remember? Oh aye, winning.

TOMMY: Yes, that is very, very true. Andy Goram may have broken my heart and Paul Gascoigne may have pissed in our jacuzzi but moving from the past to the present and looking to the future, it would be very, very true to say that the build-up to any Old Firm match is intense and it's all down to which team handles the pressure best on the day.

WALTER: That and which team has the least diddies in it.

TOMMY: How do you, as manager of Evertonfootballclub, see the match between Rangersfootballclub and Celticfootballclub going then?

WALTER: Well, obviously, particularly, at the present moment, I've been very busy with my own club and I haven't been keeping up with events at Rangers as much as I'd like. But I think, on the day, with the likes of Negri, Rosenthal, Prodan and Charbonnier in the side, Rangers have the class to beat Celtic and blow the Championship race a wee bit wide open.

TOMMY: Errr, I think it would be very, very true to say, I disagree with you, Walter. I feel that the supporters of Celticfootballclub suffered long enough. Out of the depths they have cried unto us, and it's up to the players to rise up above petty religious divisions, go to Castle Greyskull and gie the Dobs a right good doing – sportingly, of course.

WALTER: Hey, wait a minute, are there now no' more Tims in Glasgow's big Proddy team and more Proddies in Glasgow's big Tim team?

TOMMY: Errr, this could be very, very true but let's keep that to wurselves.

ONLY AN EXCUSE?

SATURDAY, 18 NOVEMBER

You have to say that Jim Jefferies seemed very relaxed, calm, at one with himself for a man who had just walked out on his job. Is this the aura of a man who has just had a huge weight lifted from his shoulders or just the aura of a man who's already got a better job lined up? Who cares? J.J. is, as Chris Robinson says, past tense.

So, who's going to replace him? Stewart Baxter has been mentioned – there's a surprise – as has Murdo MacLeod, Alex Totten, Kenny Dalglish, Graeme Souness, Robert Duvall, Mel Gibson, Al Gore, George Dubya Bush and Winston Churchill. But interestingly enough, so have the names of Sandy Clark, Craig Levein and John Robertson.

Now, if they are going down the 'Jambo connection' route, then can we throw a name into the hat? How about Maurice Johnston, a true Jambo – Hearts, he did say, were one of only a few teams he ever wanted to play for. Mo-Jo could bring some Stateside pzazz, some bare-faced cheek and a few cheap but good players to Tynecastle. And being American players, Chris Robinson wouldn't need to pay them. They'd settle for free tickets for the Tattoo and a kilt in their clan tartan even if their name was Cruz or Rabinowitz.

So, how's about it Chris, a wee bit of devilment? Go for Mo, liven up Gorgie Road and turn Tynecastle into the 51st State.

SUNDAY, 19 NOVEMBER

It's got to be the last thing Martin O'Neill or Dick Advocaat want right now and, to be honest, neither of us fancy it much either. But this week's Scotland v. Australia friendly could have turned out to be a historic occasion. For the first time, we reckon there would actually have been some Celtic supporters at a Scotland match. No, they wouldn't have been there to cheer on Scotland, they would have been there to boo Mark Viduka.

Now, sadly the player with such a delicate touch for a big man is injured and won't play. Shame. His reception was about the only thing that made this match even remotely interesting.

'STEWART MILNE'

I was going to say I thought it had turned a wee bitty chilly up here in Aiberdeen, then I remembered ma heid was as baldy as a baboon's bahooky and that's where I was feeling the draught. The Sky cameras seemed very interested in my head all the same. Not that I was bothered. I was more concerned about events on the pitch.

I couldn't believe we didn't get that obvious penalty – the one when Amoruso handled in the second half – or the less obvious one when Young Bazza tripped Stavrum. Maybe the referee thought Ferguson had connected with the ball first. Fair enough. But when young Derek Young tackled Scott Wilson and got his second yellow card, the ref took a different view even although Derek assured everyone that he got the ball first. I think he said it was the left one.

Mind you, had Mr McCurry given Aiberdeen the penalty in the first half he would have to have sent off Ferguson too and there's no way that was going to happen. He couldn't do that *and* attend the next Lodge meeting, could he? Jings, listen to me, I'm starting to sound like a Celtic supporter.

Despite the disappointment of the result on Sunday, I'm very happy with the way things are going at the club. Any day now we expect an inquiry from someone about Eoin Jess. We're coming to that time when a lot of Christmas Fayre's are needing opened and Eoin could do a job there. Mike Cormack has come in and he's doing a great job of whatever it is he does, and Ebbe's saying he needs more time again so, he's been consistent with excuses and that's something we can build on.

Winning games? Well, we actually scored a goal on Saturday. Can we not celebrate that occasion first before we start getting bogged down with controversial issues like winning.

WEDNESDAY, 22 NOVEMBER

There have been a few names mentioned since Jim Jefferies took the difficult decision to give up a rotten job at Hearts for a better job at Bradford. Steve Bruce, Sandy Clark and the inevitable Stuart Baxter are all possible candidates. On Friday you had Eric Black saying he'd been offered the job but had turned it down. He even issued an official statement to say as much, while Hearts issued an official statement of their own: 'Naw we didnae offer him the job, ken?' Whatever the truth, it would seem that Hearts are working diligently, whittling down the hundreds of applications and have now almost certainly drawn up a short list of possible, definite maybes for the job.

But the big question is, was the name of Ivan Golac on it? When J.J legged it and his job was first advertised, Ivan was one of the first applicants. What proof do we have? Well, he applies for every job going, doesn't he? But before everyone in Scottish football – except, of course, the Hearts supporters – gets too thrilled at the prospect of the Crafty Croatian's flower-smelling style of management returning to these shores, we just have this sneaking suspicion that Ivan's was one application the Jamboard just didn't take seriously.

FRIDAY, 24 NOVEMBER

One thing you have to say, they're passionate about their football up in Aiberdeen, eh? The shock announcement from inspirational boss, Ebbe Skovdahl, that he wouldn't be all that bothered if he wasn't kept on at Pittodrie has whipped up the Dons faithful into a frenzy of indifference. You have to wonder just what has been the master plan at Aberdeen all these years? If it's to take the passion out of the game, the competitiveness, the importance

ONLY AN EXCUSE?

of winning, then it has certainly worked. The place is like some sort of soccer Brigadoon. It only comes to life twice every season when Rangers come to call.

SATURDAY, 25 NOVEMBER

Interesting to read that Ranger Ronald de Boer was annoyed at having his name used on the computer game *FIFA 2001*. Having checked this game out we think Ronald should just keep his head down and say nothing because, to be quite honest, the computer version of de Boer is playing a lot better than the real one.

SUNDAY, 26 NOVEMBER

Martin O'Neill's favourite fantasy figure? How about Neil Lennon in a Celtic strip. Three or four months ago Lennon was a '£5 million-rated' player. After Martin O'Neill joined Celtic and made an enquiry for his former midfielder, he was suddenly a '£6 million-rated' player. Leicester told Martin to put his Celtic credit card away.

Fast-forward to the present day. Neil is now the '£8 million-rated' Lennon and the peroxide play-maker is still not for sale – despite the fact that Martin O'Neill says Leicester boss Peter Taylor contacted Celtic, asked them if they were still interested in buying the player and invited them to make a bid . . . which he then knocked back. Taylor said he didn't contact Celtic, then he said he did, then he said that Lennon just hadn't been performing since he signed his new improved deal – now there's a surprise – then he said Lennon was playing great.

End of story or merely the beginning? Reading between the lines, we reckon Celtic will be back in for Lennon and will eventually get their man simply because that's what the player himself wants. And what players want, players get. In fairness to Neil Lennon, he's obviously a Celtic man through and through and desperate to play for the club he loves. I mean, why else would a man on £32,000 a week be willing to take a massive pay cut to a paltry £28,000?

MONDAY, 27 NOVEMBER

Can you hear the drums Fernando? They're beating a slow death march for Ricksen, he of the exquisite, kung fu technique. The SFA disciplinary committee has hauled the Dutchman up, either for having an off-the-ball kick at Aberdeen's Darren Young that everyone saw except Mike McCurry and his assistant, or for saying he had to 'straighten Young out' on his website.

The big question is, though, if the committee are now finally going to use video evidence to nail somebody, does this mean they might even use it to clear people as well? And what about *really* bad refereeing decisions? Will they punish officials for them?

Mind you, as was exclusively revealed on *Lodge Sportscene*, new legislation coming in could change the whole face of football discipline. Seems that the European Court of Human and Footballers' Rights has announced that players unhappy with the discipline meted out to them can now take their case to court. Does this mean that everyone who gets sent off automatically appeals and it takes a year for their case to come to court – of, if there's a COSLA strike, they get off with it – thus making a mockery of the current dictatorial but fair system? Another development comes under the banner of 'freedom of speech'. If the legislation goes through, then managers will now be able to rant and rave and slag off officials with impunity. So, no change there.

TUESDAY, 28 NOVEMBER

When we read the words 'St Johnstone' and 'crematorium' in the same sentence we immediately presumed this was something to do with a revolutionary way of filling the seats at McDermott Park, but we were wrong. Apparently there is a road near to the stadium but the football fans are not allowed to use it because it passes close by the crematorium and the Cooncillors are worried that mourners might be upset by St Johnstone fans – or indeed *vice versa*.

Saints supremo Geoff Brown pointed out that the club only want supporters to be able to use the road after matches as it would be a good way of alleviating congestion – congestion, at McDermott Park, gie' us a break – and reckons you'd be talking about roughly 20 minutes to allow the St Johnstone home support to disperse.

Twenty minutes? Don't know about you, but that seems an awful long time for just ten country gentlemen in deerstalkers to stroll down a road.

'GRAEME SOUNESS'

Can I just say something here? Yeah, for sure, the boys were superb on Sunday. Amoruso, Reyna, Ferguson, Clark, they all did their bit to see off Celtic. I read that Bert Konterman had said that he thought that, over the past few weeks, the devil had been present at Ibrox. But I can honestly say I haven't been near the place.

What about Dick Advocaat, then? Superb tactics. He proved once and for all he is without doubt the second-best Rangers manager ever – although some of his signing targets I would have to disagree with. For example, everyone knows that Dick tried to sign Rab Douglas – probably right now the Celtic fans wish he had. There's mystery about the former Dundee stopper I just can't figure out. How come he's six-foot-four when he stands normal and five-foot-four when he jumps for a corner? Anyway, I know that big Rab received lots of support from fellow goalkeepers, plus a card that read. 'Thanks for giving me back my life'. It was signed 'Ian Andrews'.

So as the Rangers fans went away to get pissed and celebrate, my thoughts were already drifting towards Celtic's ultra-crucial match against Hibs. Can Celtic pull their faces out of the dirt and get back on track with a victory at Easter Road or will they crash spectacularly to a season-shattering, humiliating, never-to-recover-from defeat that will ultimately hand the Championship to Rangers? Of course, personally, I couldn't care less. I'm only interested in my own team and what's best for them. But I am faced with a dilemma over Eyal Berkovic. Do I do Celtic a favour and take him off their hands? Or do I do Rangers a favour and leave him where he is?

Incidentally, just before I go, did you happen to read about the match in Uruguay between Naçional and Peñarol? *Nine* players arrested after an on-field riot. Now that's what I call football.

ONLY AN EXCUSE?

WEDNESDAY, 29 NOVEMBER

Things about football that really do our heads in No. 367: players being booked for 'over-celebrating' a goal.

Two recent cases highlight the inconsistency in applying this daft rule. Dundee United haven't won a match all season, they're 1–0 up against Dunfermline when Craig Easton scores the crucial second. Gripped by ecstatic rapture – and possibly in a state of shock – he runs towards the long-suffering United fans to celebrate and is promptly booked for his troubles. Example two, Ron de Boer scores against Celtic, almost joins the crowd in his celebration and – quite rightly in our book – no action is taken.

If they were running to the opposition fans, flicking the Vs, making obscene gestures or using any body language that could only be interpreted as saying, 'Get it right up you', then you could understand the authorities coming down hard, but not when it's your own fans, surely? Unless, of course, this rule is really all just about the amount of time that gets wasted while the celebrations are taking place. That was certainly the case at Ibrox. Ronald de Boer did waste a fair bit of time amongst the punters, but then you know how long it takes the average Rangers fan to shake your hand.

DECEMBER 2000

FRIDAY, 1 DECEMBER 2000

Every now and again some loony comes up with some hair-brained theory, like there's life on Mars, the Loch Ness Monster definitely exists or that it would be a good idea to have an all-British international side. It's not even worth arguing about, is it? Mind you, it didn't stop a panel of experts – i.e. footie journos – from coming up with their British XI. Unbelievably there was one Scotsman in the team, Barry Ferguson. Neil Sullivan and Don Hutchison were in it too, but they're not really Scotsmen, are they?

Hot on the heels of the 'all-British' brainwave came another inspirational vision that whipped us up into a frenzy of indifference, bringing back the home internationals. Apparently there's a sponsor already in place. Who, we wonder: Horlicks?

We've not had a good 'Soccer Ace in Speeding Rap' story for a wee while now but Dundee's Juan Sara made up for that last week when it was revealed he had been clocked doing 103 m.p.h. between Edinburgh and Perth. Now, in fairness, leaving either of these two cities at 103 m.p.h. is understandable – anyone would want to get away from both of them as quick as possible. But the law is the law and Juan must pay the price for his folly. Just one thing, though. When sentence is passed, will Speedy Gonzales lift his Versace shirt to reveal the slogan 'Jesus Loves You' or 'Jesus Says Does Anybody Want to Buy a Motor, good wee runner, taxed and MOT'd, any offer considered?'

ONLY AN EXCUSE?

SATURDAY, 2 DECEMBER

It's fairly common these days for showbiz celebrities to get involved with football teams, but we can exclusively reveal that there is absolutely no truth in the rumour that Jonathan King is interested in getting involved with Albion Rovers. The story may have stemmed from the fact that King had expressed an interest in some of the Rovers' training methods.

'CHICK YOUNG'

Ho! Ho! Ho! Yes, this is totally me with the quite astonishingly sensational news. There I was on Saturday night, watching the grand final of *Stars in Your Eyes*, with lots of people pretending to be someone else, and I switched over to *Sportscene* and the Dundee/St Johnstone match, with Claudio Caniggia pretending to be Michael Bolton.

What about St Johnstone's equaliser? As the ball was scrambled away from behind the line the Saints fans held their breath. After all, the referee was Hugh Dallas so there was no guarantee he'd seen it. But, shock of shocks, the goal stood and Dundee were left to rue the barrowload of gilt-edged chances they'd blown earlier.

But what about the Old Firm? Celtic? Well, their defence has been coming in for some criticism recently. But all credit to them on Saturday, they kept it very tight for the first 57 seconds. But credit where credit is due – albeit grudgingly. Some of Celtic's play was smoother than Gordon Smith's chin and victory was secured.

But what about Rangers, the 'Gers, the Teddy Bears, the Sons of Will-yem? Stuart Dougal must be punished severely. He must never be allowed to referee a Rangers game ever, ever, ever again. OK, Christmas is coming, but did he really need to dish out all his cards at once? And sending off Classy Claudio and Superhuman Numan for basically doing what they get away with every other week at Ibrox was just scandalous. A big Teddy Bear thank-you goes to ex-Hun, Gordan Petric, who's brilliantly inept challenge on Prince Barry provided the Truth Defenders with their one chance to score which Big German Jorgy gratefully accepted. Now it's on to Euro-glory as Advocaat's Blue and White Army seek to advance into the next stage of the UEFA Cup – always, in my book, a better tournament than the Champions League.

ONLY AN EXCUSE?

TUESDAY, 5 DECEMBER

Go with the Flo would have been, we think, a good, clever name for the inevitable video that commemorates Rangers' most recent gubbing of Celtic. But Flo, although scoring, was hardly man of the match so it perhaps wouldn't be fair to name the video after him, would it? Barry Ferguson, Claudio Reyna and Lorenzo Amoruso were the top 'Gers that day but *Simply the Best, Barry None*, *Long to Reyna Over Us* and *The Grand Old Days of Lore(nzo)* just don't have quite the right ring about them. So, in the end, the video men at Ibrox opted for the rather uninspiring *Rangers' Revenge* which, we feel, represents a chickening out of what they really wanted to call it, i.e. *Get It Right Up You, Celtic*.

WEDNESDAY, 6 DECEMBER

In the week when *Coronation Street* was making all the headlines for being the country's longest running soap opera, Scottish football's very own longest running soap opera came to an end when Neil Lennon finally signed for Celtic.

Just to remind you of the chain of events, it went something like this. Leicester boss, Peter Taylor, said Lennon was playing great, then he said he was playing poorly, then he said Lennon wasn't for sale, then he said he was, then he said he wasn't. Then he set a deadline, then the deadline passed, then the deal was off, then the deal was on, then he was determined to hold on to him, then he couldn't stand in his way, then it was all off, finally, once and for all, then Neil Lennon signed for Celtic. The only thing consistent throughout the entire affair? The inconsistency of Peter Taylor.

So, what have Celtic got? Well, not since the days of Macleod,

Grant, Johnston and Shepherd has so much peroxide been in evidence. And as for the teeth, we were wondering if Lennon went to the same dentist as Macca. And that was a nice touch against Dundee on Sunday night. Playing his début in the City of Discovery, Neil turned out looking like Oor Wullie.

THURSDAY, 7 DECEMBER

One year ago Rangers beat Borussia Dortmund 2–0 at Ibrox then went to Germany, lost 2–0, then got humped in a penalty shoot-out. This year they beat Kaiserslautern 1–0 at Ibrox, then went to Germany and lost 3–0. Surely that's not just a case of not making progress, that looks like they're starting to go back the way.

'The Gaffer' is now saying publicly that he knows what's wrong with Rangers but does not want to say publicly what that is. Not that he doesn't want to, you understand. As he pointed out to Chick Young on Friday night's meeting of *Lodge Sportscene*, he feels sorry for the fans, he would like to tell them what's wrong, but he doesn't want to tell them through the media because then all the opposition would know. So, what is he going to do? Go up to every fan's house and tell them personally? Or print a full explanation in the *Rangers News*, but only if all journalists and non-'Gers fans promise not to read it? Is this all not just an enigmatic way of saying, 'There are too many diddies in our team and, yes, I am fully aware that I bought most of them.'

The fact is that Rangers could have, should have buried what is, let's be honest, an average side. Mind you, that is, of course, average in a Bundesliga-German-football-is-a-wee-bit-better-than-ours sense.

ONLY AN EXCUSE?

FRIDAY, 8 DECEMBER

Before anyone asks, no, neither of us received an invitation to Madonna's wedding. We never even got as much as a 'we don't really like you but we'll take a present off you' invitation to the reception only. Not that we're bothering, of course. We've always thought she was rubbish anyway. One interested party in all this, though, is Craig Brown. With Rocco being baptised in Dornoch Cathedral, wee Craigsie wants to know if that's him eligible to play for Scotland.

SATURDAY, 9 DECEMBER

It's one of the great mysteries in football: why so many managers have forked out so much money for Duncan Ferguson. When they're handing over the cheque to secure the services of the big man, are they really thinking, 'Maybe that's all his injuries behind him now?' Is there any bit of this guy that hasn't been injured and why is the 'will he/won't he play for Scotland' debate an issue? Craig Brown can pick him for the national side all he wants, he's never fit anyway.

It really is turning into the *Wacky Races* at Tynecastle with Darren Jackson, the Dick Dastardly of Scottish football, just one of the big names to be told your services are no longer required at Hearts. Kevin James is another one. If only Rangers had known about this earlier. They could have snapped up Kevin to play the role of 'big bloke who runs about the box' for a lot less than the £12 million they forked out for Tore Andre Flo?

SUNDAY, 10 DECEMBER

Anyone who was at Pittodrie on Saturday must have come away thinking that was the most excitement they'd seen there all season. The fact that no one was actually playing on the pitch might have had something to do with it. Everyone, ourselves included, were convinced that monsoon conditions mixed with hurricanes would be blowing the length and breadth of the country and that the entire Premier card would be wiped out, but only the New Firm's clash in Aberdeen fell victim to the weather. Both teams were probably relieved. It's not often either team can say on a Saturday, 'We didn't get beat today.'

Aberdeen we just can't get our minds round. The word is that if Ebbe doesn't make the top six – If? You've got to admire their sense of humour – then his contract won't be renewed. That's like the captain of the *Titanic* saying let's wait and see if we hit the iceberg then we'll decide what to do. Wouldn't it be a better idea to pay the man off now – Aberdeen are well used to that – and appoint Eck Black captain while there's still a chance to avoid the bottom six?

MONDAY, 11 DECEMBER

Spare a sympathetic thought for those good people of Arbroath still suffering the mother of all hangovers following a long weekend of knocking back the champagne and smokeys. We dare say beating arch-rivals Montrose in the Cup will have had something to do with it, but the main reason for celebration is, of course, the news that their long-standing world-record score – Arbroath 36–Bon Accord 0 – still stands following what looked like a serious challenge from Romania. But after checking

ONLY AN EXCUSE?

into the result – Carpati Mirsa 41–Avintol Dirlos 0 – those awfully nice *Guinness Book of Records* people announced that, as both these teams were amateur, then professional Arbroath's stunning home win back in 1885 remained the world record.

Carpati Mirsa were understandably none too pleased and promptly issued a challenge to Arbroath to play a match at a neutral venue to see who was most deserving of the title. Arbroath declined the offer after pointing out that their world-record match took place way back in 1885 and only four of the players who played in it were still with the club.

'ALAN McINALLY'

Yeah ... well ... uhm ... OK ... Mark Viduka, great player and, incidentally, a good, good great personal friend of *mein guten* self from my days in Munich with Bayern in Germany, which is just next door to Zagreb in Croatia in Australia. And the first time I saw Big Mark – or Big Marko as he was then – I said to myself, I said, 'Rambo, that big man has all the talent required to become the biggest big man of all time, or even longer in the history of big, big men in football.'

Now, I could be wrong but I very much doubt it because see ... uhn ... err ... right ... put it this way ... as a big man, I know a big man when I see one, and we're not just talking about height here. No way, bud, height alone does not a big man make. No, there's more to being big than mere height. There's stature, there's talent, there's playing for the likes of Bayern Munich. I'll say this, though. Leeds paid Celtic a paltry six million smackers for the big man and the big man's been a sensation in the big-man stakes. Rangers paid twelve million smackers for Tore Flo, who is an even bigger man than Mark, but only in a physical sense. I'm telling you, bud, if Big Flossy's worth 12, then what must Vido be worth now? And I'm telling you something else, bud, big Ozzo's performances in the Champions League will not have gone unnoticed. And I wouldn't be surprised if some of the big guns on the Continent aren't already looking to snap him up for a mega fee. He could go on to become the new Christian Vieri or, even better than that, the new Alan McInally.

ONLY AN EXCUSE?

WEDNESDAY, 13 DECEMBER

We're not sure awards are a good idea. They only seem to bring out the worst in people, and it's especially disconcerting to see your footballing heroes behaving like a bunch of luvvies at the BAFTAs. Didn't your opinion of Luis Figo – not as a player, as a bloke – dip ever so slightly when he started whingeing on about Zinedine Zidane winning the FIFA Player of the Year award instead of him. To be fair, we would both have given the award to Figo. For what he did to England alone in the European Championships he was most surely worth it. And don't forget Z.Z. was sent off twice in the Champions League – surely not the behaviour you would expect of a Player of the Year.

But Figo's mumpings were strictly second division when it came to the pomposity and sheer arrogance displayed by arguably the two greatest players the game has ever seen. Pele and Maradona. Somehow FIFA worked it that there were two Player of the Century awards and there was one for each of them. Obviously, appeasement was the order of the day, but did it work? Obviously, neither player can stand the sight of the other. Pele – who always seems to come across as a smug git who loves himself and reckons he is the greatest player ever – obviously has nothing but contempt for a crazy dude like Diego Maradona – who is also, it has to be said, not without a streak of arrogance himself and maybe would behave exactly like his rival Pele if his brains weren't so scrambled.

But it raises an interesting debate. Who was the best? Pele or Maradona? Well, put it this way. Just imagine it's a cold, frosty morning and you're playing on red ash in the Glasgow and District Superbargain Kash 'n' Karry Sunday Morning Pub League clash and you're 2–0 down to The Masonic Arms. Who would you rather have in your team, Pele or Maradona? Has to be Maradona, right?

Diego might have been 100 per cent Argentinian, but he was definitely mental enough to be Scottish. He always played with the same sort of passion and desperation that most of us play with, only he had just that wee bit more ability. He would get the sleeves rolled up and could win the match by himself no matter what the match, what the surface. Pele? He had it all, but did he have the passion? Could you see him on red ash, dribbling between the broken bottles, dogs' jobbies and fish suppers?

SATURDAY, 16 DECEMBER

Expect a BBC *Sportscene* special exclusive feature on Danish 7th Division side Hoersholm-Usseroed any day now. Why would anyone in Scotland be interested in a wee diddy team from Denmark? Because Brian Laudrup plays for them.

SATURDAY, 16 DECEMBER

Interesting to read that that world-famous cathedral of the beautiful game, the Maracana Stadium in Brazil, is crumbling because support pillars have been eroded by the amount of urine passed by supporters. All we can say is, if pish can bring down a stadium, how come Pittodrie hasn't collapsed months ago?

ONLY AN EXCUSE?

SUNDAY, 17 DECEMBER

So, Fernando Ricksen becomes the first player to be found guilty after video evidence was viewed. Read what the Rangers defender thinks of this on his new website, www.learntoshutyourgubinfuture.co.uk.

'FERGUS McCANN'

Well, what do you know. I use the phrase 'smell the coffee', and within two years you've got Starbucks and Costas popping up all over the place. I may sue them for stealing my idea.

Now, before you ask, of course I keep in touch with events at Celtic Park. I see they've just signed Suzanne Vega, that's great news. Now they can stop playing those Glenn Daly records and have Suzanne sing to the fans instead.

By the way, I see the share price is plummeting. Gee, that's a shame. And I hear UEFA have told the Old Firm that their stupid plans to quit Scotland and form a European Second Division are a 'no go'. Wow, what a surprise. And what's this? Out-of-court settlement for sacked Kenny Dalglish? I don't want to say I told you so, so just call me Mystic Fergus and we'll leave it at that.

Incidentally, I can't wait to go along to check out the latest exhibits on show at Celtic Park. I hear there are really important items on view that mean so much to all true Celtic supporters – like Steve Chalmers' Lisbon jersey, medals that were won by Celtic greats from the past and, more importantly, perhaps the greatest Celtic relic of all, my bunnet. It kind of reminds me of the story of William Tell and how he got into trouble for refusing to bow to the Emperor's hat. Well, I can assure you that I will not expect anyone to bow to my hat. A nod or a salute will do just fine.

ONLY AN EXCUSE?

MONDAY, 18 DECEMBER

An epoch ended last week when Celtic and Kenny Dalglish settled out of court and the former King of Paradise walked off with around £600,000 in his back pocket. Now, of course, legally Kenny was entitled to this, but *morally*? It will be interesting to see how the end of the 'Dalglish the Director of Football' era will affect the way Celtic fans now remember the 'Dalglish the Player' era. How will they sum up this period in Dalglish's career? Caley Thistle, 21 points behind Rangers, La Manga, 'Do you like my tan?'. Many will feel that Kenny should now hand the money back to Celtic and say, 'Here. After all, John Barnes was all my fault.' Or even, 'Here. That'll go towards making up for Raphael.' Call us cynical, but somehow we can't see that happening.

WEDNESDAY, 20 DECEMBER

Well, what about Madonna's wedding then? All the big stars were there – Rupert Everett, Sting, Mrs Sting . . . er . . . Gwyneth Palthrow . . . er . . . Madonna . . . the bloke she got married to, and one of Paul McCartney's weans. We were just wondering, though, what was going on behind the scenes and we reckon something must have gone seriously wrong. After all, here you had the biggest showbiz event of the year taking place right here in Scotland and Ally McCoist wasn't at it!

THURSDAY, 21 DECEMBER

As we've stated many times before, we are unashamed tradition-alists when it comes to when football matches should be played.

However, this fad they have in England of playing matches at 11 o'clock in the morning does have its advantages. There's something vaguely decadent about lying on the couch in your 'jammies' and bathrobe, munching on your breakfast croissant and flat sausage while enjoying a quality match like Liverpool v. Arsenal, as was the case last Saturday.

Granted that's Liverpool now beaten Manchester United and Arsenal in the space of a week, but they're not the finished article yet although you do get the feeling that they're a team on the way back. Arsenal, on the other hand, looks like a team in need of rebuilding. Both old men Adams and Seaman were missing, and the ageing Dixon, Keogh and Bergkamp all looked to be struggling. Which brings us to the Gunners' shirt sponsors. Currently they've got a deal with Sega. Wouldn't it be more appropriate if that deal was with Saga?

FRIDAY, 22 DECEMBER

With a top-class, inexpensive manager now in place and all their best players just about sold, the time was right for the King of Hearts, Chris Robinson, to announce a proposed Jambo exodus from their traditional Tynecastle home to a new, purpose-built 30,000-seat state-of-the-art stadium situated in the west of fair Edina. We've only one question to ask. Why?

SATURDAY, 23 DECEMBER

Well, well, well. Allan MacDonald has finally come out and said he should never have given Kenny Dalglish a job at Celtic Park, but as far as we know Kenny Dalglish has still to come out and say he should never have given John Barnes a job at Celtic

ONLY AN EXCUSE?

Park. Mind you, Dalglish has said very little about anything since he received his 'Pansy Potters' from his former pal. In fact, arguably the only sound coming from the Kenny camp was that of a substantial cheque being folded and placed in a wallet. Incidentally, just in case you were still wondering, the final straw in Dalglish's Director of Football Operations stint was his late arrival back from a 'youth tournament' in La Manga after Celtic had crashed out at the Scottish Cup at the feet of mighty Caley Thistle. Of course, the big question still being asked is what kind of 'youth tournament' are we talking about, football or golf?

SUNDAY, 24 DECEMBER

Now that Inverness has been officially given the status of 'city', talk is already of a change of name for their football team, Caley Thistle.

Inverness City seems a perfectly good name, but then so did Inverness Caley and Inverness Thistle. And has there ever been a name to conjure up images of silky football played on a perfect pitch more than the name Inverness Clachnacuddin? But the fact is, up in Inverness they seem to like changing their name every few years so let's just let them get on with it. Oh, and by the way, one of the names we heard mentioned as a possible was Highland Celtic. Well, we reckon that aint such a good idea. They're still suspicious enough about Culloden and its aftermath without importing Celtic paranoia up there too.

MONDAY, 25 DECEMBER

OK, so it is Christmas and at this time of year it's not unusual to break with tradition and do something a wee bit different. We've decided to give you a quiz to help you while away the interminable days of boredom between Christmas Day and Hogmanay, when you can go back to the serious bevvying again without anybody moaning.

So, here we have the *Only An Excuse?* Quiz of Quizzes for you to test your knowledge of the beautiful game.

1. What happened to Stewart Milne's wig?
   a) It blew off
   b) Chick Young nicked it
   c) It eloped with Gordon Smith's goatee beard

2. Who was the star of the movie *Gladiator*?
   a) Russell Crowe
   b) Brad Pitt
   c) Jim McLean

3. Keigan Parker is named after which famous person?
   a) Parker, Lady Penelope from *Thunderbird*'s chauffeur
   b) Dorothy Parker
   c) Fess Parker, the bloke who played Davy Crockett, King of the Wild Frontier

4. Which curry is the hardest to digest?
   a) Madras curry
   b) Vindaloo curry
   c) Mike McCurry

5. What is the proper name for a South American cowboy?
   a) Gaucho
   b) Dundee player
   c) Dundee United player

6. St Mirren have not been awarded a penalty kick all season. What should they do?
   a) Start wearing blue jerseys
   b) Start wearing the Hoops
   c) Try getting the ball into the opposition's box

7. How many Clydebank fans turned up to watch their team play Stranraer?
   a) 200,000
   b) 100,000
   c) 63.
   If you picked c) then name them.

8. Which award did Denis Law recently pick up?
   a) Turino Board of Tourism Prize for Outstanding Services to Promoting the City of Turino
   b) The Riki-Tiki-Tavi Award for Services to Mongoosery
   c) The Still-having-the-same-hairstyle-after-all-these-years Award

9. Who of the following is a good, good, great personal friend of Alan McInally?
   a) Big Augy Augenthaler
   b) Big, Big Franz Beckenbauer
   c) The entire population of the world

10. Eyal Berkovic dressed up as which character at the recent Celtic player's party?
   a) Marlene Dietrich
   b) The Invisible Man
   c) The Grinch

Answers to be printed June 2005.

'DAVY PROVAN'

Hello reader, yes reader, well reader, first up may I wish you all on behalf of me and myself a quality Christmas. For me the festive period has thrown up a very interesting question, namely what did they used to blast out the PA systems at football matches before Slade and Wizzard brought out 'Merry Xmas Everybody' and 'I Wish it Could be Christmas Every Day'. Whatever happened to 'Mary's Boy Child' and 'The Little Drummer Boy'? That's what I and I'm sure many others would like to know.

But getting back to the football. As you know, we on Radio Clyde would never criticise a professional footballer for being a diddy. We feel it is wrong to rip the piss out of someone who is, after all, only making a living. Match officials, on the other hand, already have good jobs and refereeing is just a way of making some extra cash for their holidays and extensions and things, so it's quite right to call them sheer quality diabolical disgraces at every opportunity. Most of them don't seem to know the laws of the game. OK, fair enough, most pundits don't seem to know the laws of the English language, but we speak for the punters not for the snobs who like grammar.

But if you were to ask me, I'd say that all the mad mentalness in football just now is all down to money. You've got a situation at Ibrox where a no more than exceptionally tall footballer, Flo, is being paid £25,000 a week tax free – trust a Tore to get a good deal on tax. But maddest of all is the news that Real Madrid have been offered nearly £4 million for Figo and Roberto Carlos to play *one* game for a world select against a Japan/Korea XI. Now, I'm sure I may be being a bit presumptuous here, but I reckon for a quarter of that they could get the entire Dukla Pumpherston team.

TUESDAY, 26 DECEMBER

It doesn't take place until some time in February but already corporate VIP packages are being offered for the Old Firm CIS Cup semi-final. Just shows you how important this trophy is, we can't for the life of us remember who the other two semi-finalists are. Anyway, we were checking out what's on offer and we have to say we were well impressed. So much so that we thought you might like an explanation of what each item actually means.

Champagne reception: i.e. glass of cheap fizzy vino

Three-course meal including wine, tea and coffee: Yes, you do get three chocolate mints but only with the de luxe package which costs £50 more

Corporate Gift: a surprise, but you can be sure it'll be something classy like a crystal lager decanter or a Celtic or Rangers table lighter that plays a sectarian tune when you light up your cigar

Executive transport: or, to give it its other name, a bus

Access to Executive Lounge: you get into a bar where you have to pay extortionate prices for your drinks

On top of all this, you get to meet up with former players. If you're a Celtic supporter you get a chance to meet up with, chat to, get your photo taken with, be a drunken nuisance towards and hear from, for the first time ever, the likes of Bertie Auld, Tommy Gemmell and Wee Jinky, how the Lisbon Lions won the European Cup. While if you're a Rangers fan you can tell John Greig what he got up to in the Sixties, be made sick by the smoke of Willie Henderson's big smelly cigar, and see how close you can get to Tam 'Jaws' Forsyth before he brings you down with a scything tackle.

ONLY AN EXCUSE?

Oh, and by the way, yes, you do get tickets for the match as well . . . we think.

WEDNESDAY, 27 DECEMBER

One of the things we are really looking forward to in 2001 is when Lorenzo Amoruso has completed his move to West Ham and, from the safety of the Big Smoke, has the obligatory pop at his former club. In fact, so worried might David Murray be about the big Un-Pally Tally blowing the whistle on what's really going on within the ramparts of Castle Greyskull that he might be inclined to force his former Top Hun to sign a 'you say one word about us and we'll give you the severe malky' clause in his release papers.

But purely in the interests of football, wouldn't it be great if Amo was to turn Blabbo so that we could find out what's really been going on in the Ibrox dressing-room. Who isn't talking to who? Who hates what and why? Why does who hate what, and why is he talking to him who isn't talking to who he hates, and therefore who is why is when is how? Would it be asking too much to expect a simple explanation? And what about the personal pain the big man has suffered? Losing the captain's armband, losing the burd, losing his marbles and taking to wearing those green boots. We've heard Amoruso being described by many a pundit as an enigma. Well, we've always thought an enigma – in a Scottish football sense – is how you describe someone who once played a good game and we're all waiting for him to do it again.

SUNDAY, 31 DECEMBER

Well, why not? Everyone else has been at it so here is our official *Only An Excuse?* team of the year. At first we couldn't make up our minds on what formation to go for – 4–3–3, 5–3–2, 8–0–2, 1–2–7 or even 6–3–3 Squadron – but in the end, just to keep things simple – for us mainly – we opted for 4–4–2 and here it is.

GOALKEEPER
- Robbie Winters (Aberdeen)
  Who can forget his outstanding performance in the Scottish Cup Final against Rangers.

DEFENCE
- Thomas Solberg (Aberdeen)
  No one gives the ball away in crucial areas with such aplomb.
- We couldn't agree on Valgaeren (Celtic) so we've reached a compromise with Val Singleton (*Blue Peter*)
- Franck Sauzee (Hibs)
  But only if he discards the poofy gloves he wears when it's cold. Come on Franck, it's a man's game!
- Bert Konterman (Rangers)
  Just in case we need someone to exorcise any devils that might possess the squad.

MIDFIELD
- Gary Locke (Hearts)
  'Lucky' Locke has been a revelation since he started attending the same dietician as team-mate Steve Fulton.
- Ian Ferguson (Dunfermline)
  Could have a problem with Bert Konterman.
- Scott Walker (St Mirren)

Has done really well since he left his brothers and enjoyed a successful solo career before giving up the singing to join the Buddies.

- Lee Wilkie (Dundee)
Someone to bring a bit of discipline to the team.

STRIKERS

- Jackie McQuillan (Kilnockie)
The ex-Celt, Ally McCoist look-a-like was sensational as Kilnockie shocked Rangers to win the Hollywood Scottish Cup under boss Boabby Duvall.
- Alex di Rocco (Aberdeen)
Deserves inclusion for his ponytail alone. Well, if you're going to play like a horse's arse, you might as well look like one.

SUBSTITUTES

Steven Tweed, Tommy Turner, José Quitongo, Oliver Tebily, Marco Negri, Sebastian Rosenthal, Daniel Prodan, Raphael Scheidt and the entire Aberdeen team.

JANUARY 2001

JANUARY 2001

MONDAY, 1 JANUARY 2001

This is, of course, the time for dishing out gongs to people who have done exceptionally well in their particular field, or are about to kick the bucket, and not that we're bitter or anything but we'd just like to point out that we've been overlooked – again. In fact, to be fair, Scottish football in general has been largely overlooked this time so we thought we'd like to offer a few names that we felt just might have been honoured in some small way for services to our beautiful wee game.

We're of the opinion that it's not the likes of that rower bloke who won his 32nd Olympic gold medal in a row or something who should be being honoured. It's the wee diddy people who do services like promoting the wearing of sensible footwear in Kirkintilloch who really deserve the trip to London and a vacant look from the Queen at close quarters. So forget your OBEs and your MBEs, here are the awards we think should have been handed out:

a GTF to Eyal Berkovic from Martin O'Neill
an ABS to Fernando Ricksen, in recognition of the braking system on his car
a DOB to Hugh Dallas, for helping to maintain levels of paranoia in the East End of Glasgow
a BLT to Steve Fulton – he's been looking a bit peaky lately
a UFO to Pat McGinlay, because he does look a bit like ET
a DLT to former DJ Peter Martin – the man who filled Dougie MacDonald's shoes as Radio Clyde's new shouter
a PMT to Jim Mclean – he needs to relax more
an SOS to Morton FC

ONLY AN EXCUSE?

a TNT to Alex Smith – best to get all that rage out in the open

a BBC to Chick Young, for services to puns

a GTI for Juan Sara, for services to getting out of Dundee too quickly

a PTO for Dick Advocaat – time to turn the record over

a TLC to *Sportscene*'s John Barnes who, don't forget, did take a punch in the gub for merely doing his job

TUESDAY, 2 JANUARY

There are parting shots and there are parting shots and Alan MacDonald certainly fired off a few *Guns of Navarone*-scale volleys as he vacated his office at Celtic Park last week. In a barrage of accusations not seen since *Celtic Minded* by Jock Brown just failed to win the Nobel Prize for Literature, Alan pointed the finger at just about everybody he'd had to work with in his capacity as chief exec. in Paradise. Dermot 'Sugar Daddy' Desmond, the Board, Dalglish, Wee Fergus, Joe Kinnear, Guus Hiddink – they've all been in line for a wee dig from Big Mac.

Best bombshell of all, though, was the discovery of a device in MacDonald's home which could have been used to discredit him and the club. What could that be, we wonder? Some sort of listening device or something more serious – like maybe it was one of those remote-controlled farting machines?

'CHARLIE NICHOLAS'

Weather-wise, picturesquely speaking, in terms of snowy scenes of top-drawer Christmas-card-like niceness, the elementaries were the victorious winners over the weekend. But if there is no game to be had then them that's in the authorities must let that what needs to be known be said and early so.

The Dundee/Dunfermline call-off is a point in case. You can only feel sympathy-wise, sympathetic for those Pars fans who travelled all the way south from Dunfermline to Dundee only to discover that the City of Discovery was discovered to be covered in snow in an 'Oor Wullie, yippee, it has snawed let's go up Stoorie Hill for a sna' ba' fight'-type way. At first, it has to be said, when the Dens Park groundsmen turned up and saw all the white stuff everywhere they just thought that Claudio Caniggia had sneezed.

Safety-wise, yer punter or yer fan must be taken into accountability. Ice and snow is a quality slippery surface and top of the tree in terms of arse-hurting should you skite and go on your jacksie and rightly so.

So, even if the playing grass is fine with its under-soil heating, the approaches, yer pavements, yer roads, yer staircases can be clogged snow-wise in spades and need cleared in shovels, which is ironical.

THURSDAY, 4 JANUARY

Bet you never thought you'd see the day when two biggish clubs in England would be battling it out for the signature of Lorenzo Amoruso but, over the last few days, that seems to be the case. West Ham and Fulham are falling over themselves to persuade the Pally Tally to turn his back on Glasgow, Princes Square and the nasty, critical Scottish press and come to London where the streets are paved with gold. Fresh from selling a young, confident star defender, Rio Ferdinand, Handsome Harry Redknapp is now desperate to sign an older, over-confident star defender to take his place.

If the rumours are true, then apparently Amo contacted his pal – that paragon of calm reasoned thought, Paulo di Canio – to ask him what he thought about a move to the Hammers. We have no information on what Paulo said to Lorenzo, but he must have given Alf Garnett's favourite club the hardest of hard sells because the following day word was the Big Ranger was joining Fulham.

Now to be fair, Fulham only became involved in the race after their captain, Chris Coleman, suffered a horrendous injury in a car crash. According to folk who know a thing or two about football – *and* Gabby Yorath and Barry Venison – Fulham boss, Jean Tigana, is a hard taskmaster who believes in strict adherence to tactics from his players. Is that really the kind of boss suited to Amo? Constant pelters in the Scottish press didn't manage it so all the Harrod's vouchers in the world aren't going to change the way the big man plays his football.

The Little General has been the Little Cutey in the whole affair. Dick Advocaat seems to be neither here nor there about his big, former capitano's proposed move. Does he know something that we don't, or is he already just smirking to himself when he imagines Big Amo coming up against top-class Premiership opposition on a weekly basis. The words 'found' and 'out' spring to mind.

'SIR ALEX FERGUSON'

Oh yes, proud, very proud, proud of all the pride I have in all the players I have played with throughout my career.

The one thing that never goes away is the hunger, that never leaves you, that's the one thing that's always there, that, the hunger ... and the thirst, the thirst for the hunger, that never leaves you either, nor the desire for the thirst for the hunger, that's always there as well ... nor the need for the desire for the hunger and the thirst 'cos, I tell you, keeping racehorses is an expensive wee hobby.

I still love Glasgow, oh yes, very proud of Glasgow, although it is changing. When I was flying into Glasgow Airport just the other week and we flew over the Clyde and I says to the passenger sitting next to me, I says, look at that, eh? All the shipyard workers spilling out the yards after a hard day's honest toil. And the guy says to me, 'What are you talking about? That's punters going to the carnival and the cinema complex at The Quay.' I got an even bigger fright on the way back to London, though. When we were coming in over the centre of the city I looked down and I thought we were flying over Chick Young. Turns out I was just looking at the top of the Millennium Dome.

And what about Coisty, eh? I couldn't believe that he nearly went from Kilmarnock to Morton on loan. I didn't realise the boy was still playing. The move nearly went through as well, but then Ally discovered he had some television commitments and he had to decide which was the less embarrassing, those Farmfood ads or playing for Morton. The adverts won, only just, mind.

By the way, I noticed there was a bit of speculation in the press recently linking me with a return to Aberdeen. Well, let me clear it all up once and for all. Yes, there is a possibility that one day I would definitely be very interested in returning to Aberdeen, but that would all depend on one thing – namely, me going completely aff my heid.

SUNDAY, 7 JANUARY

It used to be the sort of thing folk in pubs actually did – spent hours discussing serious matters and pondering questions that had stumped greater minds than their own like, can you name the Magnificent Seven? OK, then, let's see:

Yul Brynner as Chris, Steve McQueen as Vin, James Coburn as Britt, Charles Bronson as Reilly, Robert Vaughn as Lee, Horst Bucholz as Chico and, the one everybody forgets because he was not so much magnificent as fat and useless and only came back to help because he thought there was a bag of dosh in it, Brad Dexter as Harry.

We thought this sort of pub pastime – spending hours trying to work out the answers to pointless questions – had died out. So you can imagine our surprise when, sitting in a bar recently, we heard a group of serious-looking drinkers asking each other that very question. 'Hey, Wull, can you name the Magnificent Seven?' Wull's answer? Henrik Larsson. And he was serious . . . we think.

MONDAY, 8 JANUARY

So, Stuart Dougal says he would be quite happy to sit down and chew the fat with Dick Advocaat any time. 'Really?' think you of a Celtic persuasion, 'I thought he already did that every week at the Lodge meeting.'

Well, what do you expect? When referees start coming away with all that 'cosy chat' stuff then you really start to worry where the game is going. Let referees come out and say why they did what they did – they should be allowed to give us a laugh just as much as the next man – or let them shut their gubs and leave us to fume and speculate. But all this 'hey, let's talk' stuff is enough to give you the dry boke. We all know that referees are already under a lot of pressure, but in making this offer has Dougal not piled a huge dod upon himself? I mean, what's he going to do the next time he has a big decision to make at Ibrox, run over to Wee Dick and have a chat about it?

TUESDAY, 9 JANUARY

One bonus of the winter break came last Saturday when we got the chance to see England's version of *Sportscene* which is called *Match of the Day*. Now you can slag off, moan about, accuse of Rangers bias, accuse of Celtic bias all you want, but we'd rather have our guys than their guys any day.

Gary Lineker is rightly synonymous with potato snacks. The guy's got the personality of a packet of crisps – and damp ones at that. Trevor Brooking's posture is reminiscent of Davros, creator of the Daleks, while his mouth moves like a ventriloquist's dummy, and as for Big Alan Hansen? If he was chocolate he would keep himself in the fridge then eat himself later in the privacy of his own room while watching himself in the mirror. It's really difficult to decide what the former Jag loves most, himself or the sound of his own voice? So hurry back *Sportscene*, all is forgiven.

We don't often feel any sympathy for burglars but what about those two reprobates who picked Duncan Ferguson's house to break into at the weekend? Of all the houses, in all the villages, in all of England they picked his. What were they looking for, expensive valuables? In that case shouldn't they have tried the doocot?

Anyway, good on the big man for dealing with them in an appropriate way. The good news is the two neds have been nicked and, miraculously, after tackling them, Big Dunc didn't suffer a long-term injury and is fit to play on Saturday.

WEDNESDAY, 10 JANUARY

A few weeks ago he was Sven *Goran* Eriksson, today he is Sven *Yoran* Eriksson. Now that he is officially the failed boss of Lazio and new England manager, the press down South have been falling over themselves to sook in with the new gaffer, and the first step, we suppose, is learning how to pronounce his name properly.

Having listened to Eriksson speak, we would suggest Sven *Yawning* Eriksson might be more appropriate. He's hardly Mr Dynamic, is he? The Swedish Svengali has already said he'll be hung if he fails, but the big question is surely will he be given the chance to fail? If the English press don't give former golden boys like Hoddle or Keegan a chance, what hope for a silver-haired gentlemen from Scandinavia? We reckon many of the press down South will simply never come to terms with the fact that here's the greatest, most important, most prestigious job in world football and some Johnny Foreigner has got it. Of course, the fact that the Johnny Foreigner in question also happens to speak better English than most of them do might also have something to do with it.

All this does a raise an interesting question, though. When Craig Brown finally packs it in after the World Cup – that's the World Cup of 2020 – would Scotland possibly be interested in appointing a foreigner too? Could this work? Why not? If they guy knows his stuff, if he brings success, if he can motivate the players, why shouldn't we look to foreign parts? You might get some reservations in football terms, but you wouldn't get any of that underlying racism in some of the objections that have been voiced south of the border. Us Scots, we are proud to say, are just not like that and we would accept anyone as manager. Just as long as they're not English, of course.

'PAUL GASCOIGNE'

Way aye, man, I'm feeling right good so I am these days and I should be back playing alongside Richard Gough really soon – oh aye, we're building for the future here all right.

Anyway, I still gets a bit bored at times and I still love Scotland, so just the other day I fancied a trip North so I gives Five Bellies some dosh and says, 'Here, go and buy us a bus.' And I phones up Alex Smith at Dundee United and I asks him how my old mate Charlie Miller is getting on and Alex says fine. Then I just happens to mention I was thinking of coming up to Dundee to visit Charlie and for some reason Alex didn't seem too keen. He says to me, 'If you're thinking of coming up here then forget Dundee. It's us who'll be hiring Maradona *and* his air rifle to keep you away from Tannadice.' So, I'll maybe just give that trip a miss.

Here, what about Big Duncan and those burglars? Big Dunc says he would have come down the stairs and banjoed them earlier but he thought it was just me and some of the lads up to our antics – you know, wrecking his house for a bit of a laugh. But when he heard them threaten the most precious things in his life, his pigeon-racing trophies, well, he had to act, didn't he?

Everton, I have to admit, have not been doing too well at the moment. I'm not sure why. Could be something to do with us not scoring as many goals as our opponents, especially in games where we're playing against them. But the gaffer, Woltah, who throughout my career has been like a manager to me, says that if we keep playing the way we've been playing then we've got nothing to worry about – 'cos we'll all be sacked and Everton will be someone else's problem.

ONLY AN EXCUSE?

THURSDAY, 11 JANUARY

Lorenzo, Lorenzo, when are you going to learn to keep your gub shut? The minute you started suggesting that you were too good for the Scottish game, the Gods of Football threw a spanner into the West Ham deal and left you with not so much egg as an omelette on your face.

If the latest rumours are correct then Handsome Harry Redknapp won't be having the services of the Italian Stallion to call on as the Hammers continue their irresistible rise to the dizzy heights of mediocrity. Amo says it will be no problem for him to join up with the rest of the Rangers squad, but we're not so sure. It can't be easy walking into a changing-room knowing that your team-mates are having a right good snigger behind your back. We know he brings a lot of it on himself, but in a way we feel kind of sorry for Amo. It can't be easy going about life with the stature of Jupiter, the physique of Michaelangelo's *David* and the touch of Frank Spencer.

SUNDAY, 14 JANUARY

I'm sure we're not the only ones who have been caught up with *Popstars*, the television programme about three producers scouring the country auditioning wannabe stars to put into a manufactured pop group. The main attraction of the programme is, of course, seeing people who fancy themselves looking like complete and utter tubes as they try to impress with their singing. It made us wonder, couldn't you do that with football? Look at thousands of would-be soccer superstars for a totally manufactured, made-up football team who are only really in it for the glamour, the kudos and the dosh? Or isn't that what they've already done at Rangers?

TUESDAY, 16 JANUARY

Over the past few years, whenever a wee diddy club gets into trouble, there seems to be no shortage of blokes stepping out of the shadows to pretend they and their invisible conglomerate can do something about it before disappearing again into obscurity. It's the would-be businessman's equivalent to *Stars in Your Eyes*: 'Tonight, Mathew, I'm going to be someone with money and a vision.'

Which brings us to Stephen Brown. Did anyone, initially at least, truly suspect there was something not quite right about the waiter-cum-self-styled-saviour of Carlisle? Perhaps not, but then he looked and talked the part didn't he? The big belly and the ill-fitting suit, the moustache, the non-existent command of grammar, the looking really uncomfortable when posing like a haddy on the touchline for the local press. His credentials seemed perfect.

WEDNESDAY, 17 JANUARY

We were flicking through some old football annuals the other day and we came across that famous photo of Archie Gemmill seconds after he'd scored (arguably) the greatest goal in the history of Scottish football for Scotland against Holland way back in the 1978 World Cup Finals and we both picked up on something neither of us had noticed before. Check out Kenny Dalglish's expression and gesture towards his team-mate. It's not so much, 'Well done for scoring (arguably) the greatest goal in the history of Scottish football', as, 'You should have passed it to me, ya greedy sonso – and no maybes aye, maybes naw about it.'

ONLY AN EXCUSE?

THURSDAY, 18 JANUARY

We'd never have put *The Celtic View* in the same category as *Fiesta* or *Knave*, but apparently a group of parents are concerned that the *View* is doing as much to corrupt their young as any top-shelf scuddie book. The Parents Truth Campaign has apparently complained after adverts for condoms appeared in *The View*, the official organ of Celtic Football Club. Not being overtly familiar with this publication we haven't been able to check out the offending ad, so we're left wondering what choices were available. The Viduka (for that big man with a delicate touch)? The Larsson (scores every time)? We were also wondering if they come ready Lubo-ricated, and can you buy ribbed ones or do they only do hooped? But, of course, the biggest question of all has to be what they call them, Johnnies or Timmies?

SATURDAY, 20 JANUARY

You may be aware or, then again, you may not be aware, or then again, you may be aware but just can't bring yourself to give a toss about the transfer system row involving the European Commission, FIFA and UEFA that is about to rip football apart. We feel this is a development of such great magnitude that it is only right that we give you the benefit of our wisdom, and explain in simple terms what it's all about and what it could mean for our beautiful if ever so slightly greedy game.

QUESTION: What do the European Commission want to do to football?

ANSWER: They want players to have the same rights as ordinary, everyday workers – i.e. the right to be able to walk out on a contract after a few weeks' notice and to earn ridiculous amounts of money just like ordinary everyday workers do.

QUESTION: What are the football authorites saying about this?
ANSWER: They're saying, 'Aye, that'll be right.'

QUESTION: Why?
ANSWER: Because.

QUESTION: Because how?
ANSWER: Just because.

Right. So, that's that cleared up. Let's move on to the next stage of the debate.

QUESTION: What are FIFA and UEFA doing to sort it all out?
ANSWER: Arguing with each other.

QUESTION: And what did they come up with?
ANSWER: A fudge. Or was it a caramel? No, it was definitely a fudge.

QUESTION: Didn't FIFA, though, come up with a solution of their own?
ANSWER: Correct. Their solution being to give the European Commission everything they asked for.

QUESTION: What was UEFA's response?
ANSWER: To challenge FIFA to a square go.

QUESTION: Who won?
ANSWER: The fight hasn't taken place yet. They are still looking for a neutral bike shed to fight behind.

QUESTION: Isn't this all just a racket so that there will be more money available for players wages?
ANSWER: Of course.

ONLY AN EXCUSE?

And there you have it. So, next time an informed debate on the subject of Bosman II and all it's ramifications crops up down your local, you'll have all the answers.

SUNDAY, 21 JANUARY

It caused a sensation and a fair bit of controversy too because – shockerooni! – the hoops on Celtic's new strip don't go all the way round. So, you would have to say that, technically speaking, they're not really hoops then, are they?

This has caused a wee bit of a stooshie, with official spokesmen for various supporters' associations coming out of the woodwork to express their dismay. Of course, if they really feel so badly about these heretical tops there's one thing they can do, don't buy them. But can you honestly see that happening?

'WALTER SMITH'

Well, obviously, particularly, at the present moment, it was great to come back up to Scotland for Ye Olde Old Firm match at Ibrox Stadium on Sunday, although I have to say I just feel that, obviously, the organisers made a big mistake. All those young kids present and not even so much as a warning on the ticket that Davy Dodds would be playing.

But it just shows you how big the Old Firm are when even with a friendly match the bookies are taking bets on it. Mind you, I have to say, obviously, I only found that out after Bruce Grobbelaar had phoned up looking for a game.

I was particularly shocked when Rangers lost the first goal, although quite happy that Alan McInally scored it because it gave him something else to talk about other than his days with Bayern in Munich with Bayern in, obviously, Germany later that night when we hit Vicky's. But, at the present moment, what can you say about Coisty? Jammy or what? Of course, he had the advantage of still playing and his electrifying inertia tore the Celtic defence apart. He also had the advantage of having laryngitis. None of the Celtic defence wanted to catch it so they gave him a wide berth.

Obviously somebody who everyone thought might be there but wasn't was Paul Gascoigne. Unfortunately, at the present moment, Gazza is suffering a shock injury. It was a shock because it happened on the training ground and, let's face it, it's not very often you find Gazza there. But getting back to the game itself, OK, we won 4–1, gave Celtic a right good doing, but I suppose we cannot claim total victory after Celtic pulled a clever flanker on us and didn't play Peter Grant. To have seen Peter's face after a score like that would really have been the icing on the currant bun.

ONLY AN EXCUSE?

FRIDAY, 26 JANUARY

If – and it's looking a bigger 'if' by the day – somebody does come in for him and Lorenzo Amoruso does leave Ibrox sooner rather than later then we think we know who Rangers could get to fill the void, Big Darius from *Popstars*. If you've been watching *Popstars* then I'm sure you'll agree this guy is the biggest ba' heid in the entire glorious history of Scottish ba' heidedness.

That's why he'd be perfect to take over from Amo. Roughly the same height and build as the legendary 'better than all the rest' Italian Stallion, Darius might not, we suspect, be the greatest player in the world, but once the Ibrox faithful saw and heard his version of Britney Spears' 'Hit Me Baby One More Time', they'd forget about Amo forever.

So, how's about it Darius? Never mind healing the world through your music, you're place is at the heart of the Teddy Bears' defence.

SATURDAY, 27 JANUARY

OK, fair enough, so *Beano* create a character obviously based on Claudio Caniggia called Claudio Poserello and we all have a wee titter. Then *Beano*-makers, DC Thomson, announce they have bought shares in Scottish Radio Holdings, the company that owns Radio Clyde. Is there something going on here? Does DC Co. intend expanding the range of their mickey-taking? Could the stars of *Super Scoreboard* be the next target? Will Paul Cooney and the team suddenly start appearing thinly disguised as Lord Snooty and his Pals or the Bash Street Kids?

And what about Dick Donnelly? We've always said that if Paw Broon had a voice it would be exactly the same as Dick's. Talking of the *Broons*, stick a moustache on Horace and he'd be the double of Hugh Keevins. Is there something Maw has been keeping quiet about all these years?

SUNDAY, 28 JANUARY

So, Gary Locke has gone to Bradford? Great move by Jim Jefferies. Apparently the physio at Bradford has been complaining about being lonely. Locke's arrival virtually guarantees there will be someone in the treatment room nearly every day.

'KENNY DALGLISH'

You asked me about John Barnes in a way that suggests that I'll try to dodge the question, but I can assure you I won't. You call it as you ask it and I'll answer it as I see it. Now that we've got that sorted out all I want to say is, I feel a lot's been said about John Barnes, no' just by me but by other folk as well, and some of them have said good things and others have said no' such good things but all I would say is, I think it was terrible what Jim McLean did to him.

What? No' *that* John Barnes? What other John Barnes is there? Oh you mean *him*? Well, what can I say? I appointed him, that's true, but on the day he walked into the manager's office at Celtic Park I said to him, 'John, I just want to offer you one piece of advice. Whoever you want to buy in the whole world is up to you. Sign anybody you want, except for anybody called Scheidt, Berkovic, Kharine or Tebily.' Now what can I do if he chooses to ignore me? Stephane Bonness, who's he? Do I know what he looks like? Nobody does. Stephane Bonnes is a Celtic myth.

By the way, don't forget all the bad luck we had. We had to go almost a full season without Henrik Larsson and a whole season *with* Vidar Riseth. When Henrik got injured I said to John, 'What about a replacement?' He said, 'de Ornelas?' I said, 'Dae something.' So he did, he signed up Ian Wright.

Now, a lot has been said about that, but after his adverts, his television shows and his public appearances, Ian Wright was totally committed to Celtic, and you can say what you like, he was the best badge-kisser the club has ever had. But, getting back to what I was saying earlier, I would just like to make it perfectly clear that I had nothing to do with any of the signings – apart from Petrov and Petta, all the rest were Barnesy's.

Would I ever consider moving back into management? Depends on the job. The Scotland job after Craig chucks it in in 2020? Maybes aye, maybes naw. All depends on what the transfer budget is.

WEDNESDAY, 31 JANUARY

Does James Richardson have the best job in the world? Not only does he live in Italy and get to go to all the big matches in Serie A, he also gets to interview all the top stars and, when he's doing his review of the newspapers, he always has a big fancy dessert on the table next to him. And talk about informative. For years we thought Milan, Milano, AC Milan, Inter Milan, Inter and Internazionale were six different teams. Now, thanks to wee Jamesie, we know better.

They even have better scandals than us in Italy. While we get all excited about motoring offences and rammies in kebab shops, the Italian authorities get to deal with things like passport scams and internet prostitution rings. Ten Inter Milan players were recently accused of securing the services of 'bad women' by computer. Whatever happened to just picking them up in a club?

Then there's the passport scandal and no, we're not talking about dodgy photographs. You see, it seems that Italy are still living in the Dark Ages with some 'only allowed to play a certain number of foreigners' rule still being enforced. To get round this, many clubs encourage their overseas players to discover an Italian grandparent, thus enabling them to get hold of an Italian passport and so no longer be classed as a 'foreigner'. First of all Argentinian Veron and now Uruguayan Recoba has been accused of not being entirely truthful when it came to revealing in his passport application from where at least one of his grandparents came from. If it's revealed that these guys should not have been given Italian passports then it could turn out that both their clubs, Lazio and Inter, have at times been playing too many foreigners in their side and both, therefore, could face points deduction as a penalty.

ONLY AN EXCUSE?

Naturally the Italian football authorities are none too pleased about this and have promised a full investigation. All the same – and you can call us cynical – somehow we just get the feeling that possibly these two very big clubs might just get off with it. Whatever the outcome, this issue does highlight one of the fundamental differences between Italian and Scottish football. Here they are more interested in how old your granny is rather than where she came from.

FEBRUARY 2001

THURSDAY, 1 FEBRUARY 2001

Football is a hard game. Sometimes ability or your uncle being the manager, isn't enough. Sometimes you look for that little – or big – confidence booster that will give you an edge. Now anybody who has played football, or indeed perhaps any sport, will know where we're coming from when we say that apart from a chosen few whom the gods have endowed disproportionately, most of us – if really pushed – just might admit to, at least once in our lives, thinking about sticking something down the front of our shorts to give us more of a manly bulge. Purely to psyche out the opposition, of course. And what's wrong with that? Women have Wonderbras, why don't men have Wonderpants? Anyway, last week some poor bloke just went too far at his club and got caught. Mind you, a cucumber down the shorts is slightly more threatening than a rolled-up sock. Thing is, though, he was charged with breach of the peace. Shouldn't the charge have been piece in the breeches'?

Celtic gaffer, Martin O'Neill, was recently said to be looking at one Paulo Rink. Rink seems an interesting character for three reasons:

(1) Rink has had a fall-out with his club.
(2) His *oberstumbahnfuhrer*, Berti Vogts, has recommended him to Celtic.
(3) Rink is Brazilian-born.

Rink also seems a bad idea for three other reasons:

(1) Does this mean he's a troublemaker.

ONLY AN EXCUSE?

(2) Is this Vogts' revenge for not getting offered the Celtic job?
(3) So was Raphael Scheidt.

FRIDAY, 2 FEBRUARY

There's Ajax. One of the most famous clubs in the world with one of the most impressive stadiums in the world and their fans are not happy. The pitch, they say, is a disgrace and the cause of many poor results this season, so they took matters into their own hands and staged a protest. On to the pitch they marched in their clogs with two cows. Obviously the point being made was something along the lines of the pitch being more like a meadow than a football pitch. Well, here's the good news. St Mirren boss, Tom Hendrie, is interested in signing one of the cows as cover for Tommy Turner.

SUNDAY, 4 FEBRUARY

Watching Sky's coverage of the Hearts/Celtic match fair took us back. When the snow was falling heavily making events on the pitch indistinguishable, it reminded us of the 'Sixties and the halcyon days of *Scotsport* when every match they covered looked like that. In fact, at one point we switched the television picture to black and white for reasons of pure nostalgia. The snow, it seemed, got everywhere on Sunday night, even the studio. It looked like Whitey had some of the white stuff on his head, or has he just been cutting back on the Grecian 2000?

Henrik Larsson is without doubt the Annabel Chong of Scottish football – he just can't stop scoring. But unless he's very careful he could get himself into trouble. Look at Juan Sara. Every time he scores a goal he whips up his jersey to reveal a biblical message of peace and love. On Saturday he scores a goal, does what he always does and gets booked for his trouble. Later in the match, Juan Sara turns a bit of a Juan Quer when he deliberately handles the ball, picks up a second yellow card and is sent off. Incidentally, he ran very fast up the tunnel. Maybe he forgot where he was. Back to Henrik. When he scores a goal he sticks out his tongue. How rude. What kind of example is this to be giving to our kids? But should he be booked for doing it? Of course not. However, rest assured there will be, out there right now, a referee looking to make a reputation for himself by doing just that.

'GRAEME SOUNESS'

Can I just say something here? Yeah for sure, I know who I want in my team for the big push. I want my kind of player, guys like I was but, unfortunately, Rob Roy won't let me talk to Chic Charnley so I've had to go for Eyal Berkovic instead. I told Eyal that when he comes here I'll give him all the help he needs to settle, to regain his fitness and, most importantly, to write an anti-Celtic rant for the tabloids.

You just have to know how to deal with Eyal. You have to know when to put an arm round him, when to take him to one side, when to threaten to sign John Hartson. Do all these things and you'll get a great player, a player who can win you a game – only when he can be arsed, of course.

I hear there was a bit of bother at the Rangers/Aberdeen match last week. Surely not? I can't understand how there are still problems with that fixture given the strenuous efforts the press and media make to take the tension out of it by printing photos of previous flashpoints at every opportunity. Great stuff.

I didn't get a chance to see the Rangers/Dunfermline match, but I'm sure Ian Ferguson must have been very disappointed to be left out of the Dunfermline team. Yeah, for sure, I would have to question Pars boss, Jimmy Calderwood's decision to do that. Denying one of his own players the right to hear the Rangers fans singing, 'Fergie, Fergie give us the sash', showed great lack of understanding. But, of course, the big one comes next Sunday at Celtic Park. *The* Old Firm match of the season and the one that could really decide it. If Rangers win, then it's down to six points and 'game on'. If Celtic win then it's a League not worth winning anyway. But one thing you can be sure of. As a true Rangers supporter, I'll be present and making my voice heard – just as long as a television company pays me.

TUESDAY, 6 FEBRUARY

To be or not to be, pay per view? That is the question. The answer goes something like this. If you want it, pay for it. If you don't, then don't. Simple as that.

Let's be honest, it's only really been introduced to fleece Old Firm fans even further, so why is everyone getting so upset about it? The St Johnstone/Celtic game you can perhaps understand. Only so many Celtic fans can travel to the game: a lot back in Glasgow would want to see it: stick it on the box but make them fork out for it. The gods of football, however – or maybe it was a voodoo spell conjured up by some Rangers fans – sent down a warning in the shape of an impenetrable fog-bank and the experiment flopped.

Then comes Saturday's Rangers/Dunfermline match at Ibrox. Most people who *really* want to be there will be or, at least, would be if the pay-per-view experiment doesn't mean switching the kick-off time to 12.55. What about folk who were out on the batter the night before? 12.55 is the middle of the night for them. No, sorry, bad enough football matches switching from Saturday to a Sunday, but ordinary League matches kicking off Saturday lunchtime? Sacrilegious.

With Big Joos out for either six weeks, the rest of the season or the next five years – depending on which report you read – the opportunity presents itself for one of the Celtic fringe defenders to push for a place. Now, at last, we might get a wee bit closer to discovering the answer to one of the most perplexing questions connected with Celtic Park. Ramon Vega or Stephane Mahe: which one's got the biggest nose?

ONLY AN EXCUSE?

According to our sources there was a man spotted around Ibrox Stadium on Saturday selling what he was referring to as 'Erra Daniel Prodan videos'. We immediately wondered how anyone could issue a video of a man who didn't play a single game for a club? However, our source has since further revealed why the aforementioned salesman was referring to his merchandise as 'Daniel Prodan' video. They were blank ones.

We're not saying it won't matter on the night – or the day after, in work places across Scotland – but the League Cup Semi-Final does pale somewhat when compared to Judgement Day 327, Soccarmageddon IX, Shocky VI, the Old Firm League match on Sunday. If Celtic win it then that could be it. If Rangers win it then that could no' be it. And if they draw then that could maybe still be it but also might not be.

Hugh Dallas. Interesting choice of referees. This will be Shug's first Old Firm match since someone tried to turn his head into a piggy bank nearly two years ago. Now, of course, he's not going to get everything right and he's never going to please everybody, but just let's hope a bit of common sense prevails and come Monday morning Hugh Dallas isn't going through the *Yellow Pages* looking for a glazier.

WEDNESDAY, 7 FEBRUARY

Continuity announcers, funny job that. That's those disembodied voices that you hear between television programmes telling you what's coming on next. They provide a great service for folk who are just stupid or are too mean to buy a newspaper.

Anyway, it seems an easy job but, probably due to boredom, mistakes do creep in. For example, did anyone happen to hear the one last Wednesday night? 'And now highlights of tonight's FA Cup replays with Richard Wilson.' *Richard* Wilson? I don't beee-liieeeeve it! Still, in fairness to the announcer, she was a woman and what do they know about fitba'?

Is Bobby – sorry – Sir Robert Charlton all right? There he was last week at a press conference to announce the deal involving the New York Yankees and Manchester United and he sat there, waxing lyrical about what a great club Manchester United were and what a great history they have and what a great game football is, and he *didn't* start crying. Not like Sir Bob, at all. We're definitely a wee bit worried. That sort of restrained behaviour is just not like him.

THURSDAY, 8 FEBRUARY

JudgeMental Day: Part One

Hampden Park, CIS Cup, the second Semi-Final.

You could tell just by looking at him that Jim Delahunt knew there was someone at the window behind him. All he could do was hope the gestures being made weren't too obscene.

For some strange reason – perhaps because it was only a wee diddy Cup Semi – everyone seemed to be suggesting this might be a quiet game. Aye, that'll be right. The minute the wee Rangers mascot looked straight at the camera and kissed the badge on her jersey you sensed maybe the experts had called this wrong.

One pundit had opined that, no matter what, Advocaat, the Little General, always pulls a tactical master stroke before a big game. What was his tactical master stroke this time, we wonder? Robert Malcolm or Tugay and Ferguson constantly getting in each other's way? For Celtic, Rab Douglas was missing but replacement Jonathan Gould made sure he wasn't missed by making a meal of some of the crosses.

The first two goals. Say what you like about Vega but for a guy with such a big nose he isn't afraid to use the nut, and Sutton didn't hang about with the rebound. Then Larsson scored. Did he foul Robert Malcolm? So far only one person has come out and said he did, Robert Malcolm.

Anyway, it's 2–0 to Celtic. Time for Rangers to do something about this, but referee Willie Young beat them to it. The spot-kick awarded for Scott Wilson leaning back and falling on his jacksie must be, arguably, the softest penalty ever given in the history of soft penalties. The one for Larsson falling over the ball comes a close second.

As the match skittered to an end what else could Rangers do but take offence at Bobby Petta's alleged showboating. Showboating? Wasn't that what Jim Baxter did to England back in '67 at Wembley? What Choirmaster Graham Roberts did in that other infamous Old Firm match? What Kanchelskis did against Ayr United, standing on the ball and looking to see what was happening? What Willie Johnston used to do, what Jimmy Johnstone used to do, what Tommy Gemmell, Willie Henderson etc. etc. etc. used to do. Showboating? Didn't that used to be called 'taking the piss'? How come it was OK back then but it's so controversial now? Come on. Let's call a spade and taking the piss, taking the piss and let us celebrate a great Scottish footballing tradition.

Almost predictably, the cameras missed it, but it did give Willie Young the chance to show that he has not just yellow cards in his pocket. As the experts had predicted, a nice calm Old Firm match.

FRIDAY 9 FEBRUARY

Scotsport really pulled out all the stops for the CIS Cup Semi-Finals. Kilmarnock v. St Mirren. On the pundit's bench we had Billy Stark (because of his Kilmarnock connection). Tommy Burns (because of his Kilmarnock connection) and Mark Hateley (because . . . er . . . because they always get Mark Hateley). Jim Delahunt – complete with Hughie Green raised eyebrow – gave it the hard sell, but really this was a bit of a no contest. St Mirren were so bad they made Gus MacPherson look like Roberto Carlos as Killie thoroughly deserved their victory.

Highlight of the night? No, not Craig Dargo's goal. That honour goes to Archie MacPherson's description of a St Mirren corner failing to make an impact after hitting 'a solid phalanx of darker shirts'. Classic.

We found out, albeit too late, that, apparently David Baddeil, Nick Hancock and Angus Deayton were lined up to be playing football at Braehead Arena last Saturday. Did it happen? Did they turn up? All we can say is, what a missed opportunity for *Comic Relief* to clean up. Wouldn't half the male population of Scotland have paid for the privilege of being on the same pitch in opposition to any one, never mind all three, of these guys?

SATURDAY, 10 FEBRUARY

We were both reading through the *Evening Times'* totally sensational 'Time Out' section on Friday when we spotted a review for a new CD, 'No Such Place' by Jim White. Well done, Whitey. We never took you for musical and there you have a new album out.

There was no mention of any of the song titles so we were left to speculate. How about some self-penned songs like, 'Laudo, Laudo, How Come You're So Good', 'What a Character We Have in Coisty' or Whitey's own tribute to Fatboy Slim, 'Right Here, Right Now, Right Mate'. You like musicals? How about extracts from the show that gave Jim his big break *Scotsport*? The show was called *Arthur and His Amazing Technicolor Sports Jacket*. Then again, maybe it's not *the* Jim White we're talking about. Ah well, music's loss.

SUNDAY, 11 FEBRUARY

JudgeMental Day: Part Two

All the pre-match talk was of players needing to behave them-selves and Hugh Dallas. It was difficult to gauge who was under more pressure, the players or the referee. Going into this match Rangers had something to prove, that they were still Championship material, and Ricksen had something to prove, that he was aff his heid. What is it about Fernando? He's got the eye of the maddie. Just one look at him and you knew what kind of game he was going to have.

The first half was all Celtic. Rangers really struggled until they received that massive boost of having Ricksen sent off and playing the entire second half with ten men. Advocaat must have delivered what must have been a rousing speech along the lines of, 'Unless you start playing, you'll be out of Ibrox by the end of the season', because Rangers were markedly better in the second half. Even so, there were still only two real moments of panic for the Celtic support, when Agathe headed Konterman's shot off the line, and when Tebily came on for Mjallby.

At this point, on behalf of all amateur footballers everywhere, we'd like to thank Jorg Albertz for kicking the ground. It's reassuring to see that even top professionals can make that mistake too.

A word about the referee? For all the praise heaped upon Mr Dallas, you have to say he did miss what looked a fair shout for a penalty. With the ferocity of Bambi, Tore Andre Flo attempted to break free and set himself up with a scoring chance, but Chris Sutton's cuddle definitely seemed to hold him back.

Performance of the day? Has to go to Graeme Souness in the role of 'distraught Rangers supporter'. BBC Scotland should put him forward for a BAFTA. Without taking anything away from Celtic, he blamed the Champions League, the crowd, injuries, the weather, tactics, the government, the Euro, and what's that word 'Bossing' he kept using? Something to do with the designer suit he was wearing?

'DAVY PROVAN'

Hello reader, yes reader, well reader, what about Henrik Larsson? Wasn't it incredible how he was able to hit his shot off Jorg Albertz' leg then control the rebound before slipping an inch-perfect deliberate pass through for Thommo to score the easiest of goals from a position he could easily have missed from had he been Harald Brattbakk. Sheer quality, poetry in motion.

Yes, you've got to hand it to Henrik. He's some man, even though – and I find this hard to believe – he wasn't voted Man of the Match. I tell you, if I'd been there, though, there's a fair chance he would have been. What do the BBC know about football anyway?

You know, whenever there's an Old Firm match, punters come up to me and say, 'Davy, wee man, you've played in a Kilmarnock/Ayr match, you've played in a Celtic/Rangers match, just what is the greatest club match in the world?' And my answer is always the same. The Old Firm, for its sheer passion alone it has got to be *the* greatest club match in the world. OK, there is the Milan derby, the Manchester derby, the Liverpool derby, the Madrid derby, the Istanbul derby, the Rio derby, the Buenos Aires derby, the Munich derby, the Paris derby and the Blantyre derby, but they only have football and blind hatred to call upon. In Scotland we've got the football and blind hatred but we've also got the venom, the vitriol, the anger, the bigotry and the sectarianism, and they just can't take that away from us. No, make no mistake, we're special *and* some.

But can I just say there are still a few more issues left to be resolved in this campaign. Extremely pressing and crucial questions still need to be asked, like will Celtic now go on to win the treble? Can Rangers catch Hibs? And, most importantly, how many more 'Man of the Match' bottles of champers will Henrik Larsson pick up before the end of the season?

WEDNESDAY, 14 FEBRUARY

The recent controversial team photo of Arbroath certainly brought a whole new meaning to the phrase 'spot the ball'. Kevin Fotheringham's flash of inspiration certainly gained the club a notoriety they've never known before. We feel, though, the whole affair has been blown all out of proportion. Possibly Kevin, in keeping with the fishy tradition of the town, was simply displaying an eel of the one-eyed variety he was particularly proud of landing. Whatever. The club certainly acted swiftly. They sold Fotheringham and categorically denied the club had considered changing their nickname from the 'red' to the 'purple' lichties.

THURSDAY, 15 FEBRUARY

Football is once again in danger of becoming the darling of the chattering classes. Ben Elton and Andrew Lloyd Webber, a right pair of smart asses, and their musical based on football, *The Beautiful Game*, have just picked up the Critic's Circle Theatre Award. Now, to be absolutely honest, neither of us have seen this show and therefore cannot confirm or deny it's a follow-up to their other footie musicals, *Aspects of Love Street*, *Fanta of the Opera* and *Superstar? Jesus Christ*. Nor do we know if any of the songs really do have titles like 'I Don't Know How to Clog Him', 'Another Boot Room 'n' Another Ball', and 'Don't Shy to Me, Argentinian'. But the idea of two guys who really know their football, guys like Messrs Elton and Webber, interpreting the subtle nuances of fitba' through cheesy tunes and smartypants words is well . . . er . . . totally beyond our comprehension. Maybe we need to check it out before we slag it off further. Anybody like to send us a couple of tickets?

ONLY AN EXCUSE?

SATURDAY, 17 FEBRUARY

It's a mystery that's up there with the Abominable Snowman, the Loch Ness Monster and How to Remove the Wrapper from a Kraft Cheese Single and it's this: how come Ebbe Skovdahl is so ridiculously popular with the Aberdeen fans? Does he give them money? Does he buy them pints? Does he frighten them with stories of Roy Aitken coming back to replace him? Anyway, the Dons fans are said to be delighted that the man who's turned their team from a bottom-of-the-League side to a third-bottom-of-the-League side has extended his contract and will be staying on for another stab at mediocrity. Is this the same Aberdeen that Fergie used to manage?

SUNDAY, 18 FEBRUARY

OK, so they tanned the mighty County up in Ross, but lots of questionmarks hang over Rangers in the wake of their defeat at Celtic Park. Chairman David Murray steps into the limelight and states the obvious. Many of the Rangers players are just not good enough. Who was he talking about? Flo? Konterman? Ricksen? Miller? Johnston? Who bought them again? Furthermore, Murray would neither confirm nor deny that Tina Turner had been approached to record a new song called 'Simply the Second – or Third – Best'. And what about Advocaat? Will he stay or will he go? If he does go then can we suggest the 'Gers go for a man with a passion for what he does and with a knowledge of the Rangers tradition. So how about Gordon Ramsay? Well, they've tried a Little General how about a Little Chef?

MONDAY, 19 FEBRUARY

Paranoia corner

Who does Barry Nicholson play for? It is Dunfermline, isn't it? It was Dunfermline he scored the late equaliser for last Saturday, right? So what's all this about never having played against Celtic when he was a Ranger and how this made up for the disappointment of his beloved Teddies going out of the CIS Cup?

Add those comments to that incident a few weeks back at Ibrox when Nicholson was clean through with only Klos to beat and – whoops! – he chips it into the keeper's arms. Makes you wonder.

Oh, and by the way, the *big* talking point at East End Park, the Ian Ferguson bobbling ball being blasted into the Celtic fans incident. Did we miss it or did *Lodge Sportscene* forget to show it? Makes you wonder even more.

'FERGUS McCANN'

This is Fergus McCann saying to all my Celtic *amigos*, hi, *bonjour*, *wilkommen*, *buenos dias* and wanna loan of a few million smackers? Or how, about a thin dime?

What is happening to the meal ticket I loved? When I was there there were no debts, no players, no trophies and no hope. Now? They've got big debts, big players, big chances and big hopes, but is this what the supporters really want? I think I know the Cel'ic fans well enough to have the confidence and cheek to speak for them in saying, no, I bet you it isn't. What use is glory without economic stability?

By the way, just what is going on at Cel'ic Park these days? Isn't it about time somebody smelled the Kenco? Look at the carry on with the new un-hooped jerseys. The Board have shown their contempt for the fans by not listening to their views before pressing on with this controversial move. If I'd still been in charge I'd have listened to the fans first before completely ignoring them and doing what I wanted.

Incidentally, while I have this platform, can I just say a few words about proposals for the new transfer system? Of course it's not going to work and why should it? A player surely must retain the fundamental right to be allowed to do whatever he wants and be able to walk away from a legally binding contract whenever it suits him. The sooner the authorities embrace this concept the sooner some progress will be made. There, a little bit of sarcasm. See, I do have a sense of humour after all.

WEDNESDAY, 21 FEBRUARY

The latest unfolding chapter in the Airdrie story? Don't believe a word of it, all porkies. Only we can exclusively reveal what's really happening. OK, are you sitting comfortably? Then we'll begin.

The mystery man waiting in the wings to snap up the Diamonds at a bargain price is none other than Montgomery Burns, owner of the nuclear plant at Springfield and boss of Homer Simpson. The multi-multi-millionaire is going to buy the club, sell all the players into slavery and tear down the Shyberry just to wind up the Airdrie fans or, alternatively, donate it to Albion Rovers just to wind them up even more. Meanwhile, Don King has declared his interest in promoting a square go between Steve Archibald and Blair Nimmo in Las Vegas, behind the bike sheds at the Sands Hotel. Andrew Lloyd Webber, meanwhile, fresh from his success with *The Beautiful Game*, has been in touch with Jim Traynor, asking if he'd like to be the librettist on a new footie-based musical he's writing about Airdrie called *Know Your Onians*.

Now, I bet you don't believe us. We bet you think it all sounds just too daft. Well, OK then, ask yourself this. Is it any dafter than what has really been happening?

FRIDAY, 23 FEBRUARY

Surprise, surprise, Duncan Ferguson is back on the treatment table again. A fractured shoulder-blade is the latest injury to blight the Bird Man of Alkaseltzer. Everton also pointed out that this is an injury he picked up a few weeks ago playing at Leeds and not, what a lot of folk are probably thinking, when trying to fly off the doocot roof with his pigeons.

ONLY AN EXCUSE?

SATURDAY, 24 FEBRUARY

What is it about footballers? They're always dressing up. Case in point? The sneaky pics taken at a party in Jackie MacNamara's house then passed on to the press. Top snap was Henrik 'The Hitman' Larsson dressed up as Bjorn 'The Hitmaker' Ulvaeus of Abba. Or was it Benny? Or does it matter? Wonder if he sang 'Fernando' or if he left that to Bobby Petta?

According to the article other 'celebrities' present included Freddie Mercury, Cher, Dolly Parton and the Spice Girls. Who could have been dressed as who, we wonder? Cher? Got to be Ramon Vega; he looks good in a skimpy mini. Dolly Parton? How about on-loaners Raphael and Berkovic? They've been a right pair of diddies in their time at Celtic Park. Freddie Mercury? Well, Neil Lennon's certainly got the teeth. But who could have been the Spice Girls? We can only think of Tommy Johnson as Ginger and Oliver Tebily as Scary. Or should that be Oliver Tebily *is* scary?

SUNDAY, 25 FEBRUARY

Quite an entertaining double whammy Sky had on offer on Sunday afternoon starting off with Man Yoo v. the Gooners. If there was one word that summed up Manchester United which would it be. 'Rich'? 'Smug'? How about 'ruthless'?

Did they hump their nearest rivals or what? Sir Fergie himself said that he thought the difference was in the penetration – perhaps the right word to use given Arsenal's goalie, David Seaman. With that hairstyle he's looking more like a porn star every day. So, congratulations to Manchester United, worthy Champions once again.

Then it was time for the Worthington Cup. The Millennium Stadium looked superb and the atmosphere did justice to a great big, wee diddy Final.

In the studio we had Kenny Dal – who could hardly contain his indifference – while Frank Worthington – he must be doing well, he's got a cup name after him – looked like he thought he was going to an Elvis convention.

Robbie Fowler's goal was worthy of winning any final, and would have, but for a rash tackle right at the death which gave the Blues a penalty that was duly scudded home. Actually, Birmingham should have had another penalty in the first period of injury time, but the ref chose not to point to the spot for the biggest stonewaller you've ever seen not given in the history of stonewall penalties. Honestly, if there was a *Guinness Book of Stonewall Penalties*, this would be on p. 1.

The last fifteen minutes were superb as both teams obviously decided, 'Penalties? Aye, that'll be shining bright', and went for it big time. The goal never came, the penalty shoot-out did, and Liverpool won.

By the way, those great Liverpool fans who were singing jubilantly at the end, were they the same Liverpool fans we saw with faces like sheets, heads in hands, worried sick when it was 1–1? You'll never boke alone? Incidentally, when the dignitaries were being introduced, we heard the name 'Keith Harris' being mentioned. Well, can we just say we looked really hard and we didn't see him or Orville the duck.

'DENIS LAW'

Happy birthday to me,
Happy birthday to me,
Happy birthday dear Denis, Happy birthday to me.

Well, you know, as I say, yes, it's true, the Lawman celebrated a birthday recently – last Saturday to be exact. Go on, have a guess what age I am? 40? 45? 50? No, I'll let you in on a secret. Unbelievable as it may seem, I, Denis Law, the Mongoose, am an unbelievable 61 years of age. No, I can't believe it either. I think it's got something to do with my hairstyle never changing in over 50 years.

So, what did I do for my birthday? I phoned up Bestie – who these days is more like Worstie – and I also phoned up Lord Bobby of Charlton to see if they fancied doing something really crazy like breaking open a packet of Werther's Originals and having a no-holds-barred game of dominoes. Surprisingly, I'm still waiting for them to call me back.

But, hey, listen, I was watching that Dundee/Rangers match at the weekend and I didn't realise you were getting snow up there. I just thought Caniggia had forgotten to use his anti-dandruff shampoo.

By the way, I hear they used orange balls last weekend. I was surprised when I heard that. I thought John Greig had retired. Only kidding, Greigy!

Incidentally, can I just say congratulations to my old friend, whom I've never met, Graham Rix, on getting the manager's job at Portsmouth. And to the people of Portsmouth can I just say, 'Lock up your daughters.'

WEDNESDAY, 28 FEBRUARY

Claudio Caniggia, Player of the Month, and no' afore time. Caniggia in full flight is something to behold, but even after all this time, deep down, no one in Scotland, not even Dick Donnelly, can believe he's actually playing for Dundee. We all think it's some sort of trick, that Ivano Bonetti is in league with David Copperfield and that the master of mystery, magic and illusion has conjured it all up out of thin air.

But even after all this, the Dark Blues are still struggling to make the break. The Bonetti solution? More players. Latest reports say as many as six players are about to arrive at Dens Park. There is, however, no confirmation that the six will be Pele, Cruyff, Rivera, Müller, Platini and Eusebio – all conjured up by David Copperfield, of course.

MARCH 2001

THURSDAY, 1 MARCH 2001

Sven Goran Eriksson is probably a nice man so we feel bad about not liking him now that he has taken the England job. Don't get us wrong – nothing against the English, nothing against the players, nothing against Eriksson, it's they bloody pundits we cannae stand.

We were switching between *Radio Five Live* and *Talk Sport* – down there it would seem every radio pundit is called Alan – and boy, do they like to crow about England. OK, it was Spain, but the match *was* a friendly, for goodness sake, and not, as their behaviour would have you believe, the World Cup Final. Even when a streaker came on to the match, they managed to turn this into a discussion about what a wonderful, crazy race the English are.

Wonderful and crazy, yes definitely, but don't forget prone to violence too. Some experts have memories shorter than David Hannah's hair. Incidentally, we hear that the police have decided upon a new method of dealing with streakers at sporting occasions. The idea is just to leave them alone, don't chase them, just ignore them, they'll eventually feel stupid and slink back from whence they came. Great idea, but wouldn't just giving them a right good kick up the arse be better?

SUNDAY, 4 MARCH

Rangers are playing like champions. No, seriously, they are. For the last two weeks they have been absolutely rotten and still managed to win the three points. So, come on, credit where credit is due.

ONLY AN EXCUSE?

Something doesn't seem quite right with the Teddies, though. Team spirit seems to be missing, so Rangers do what they always do when faced with a situation like this: become linked with Eoin Jess again and have Barry Ferguson start talking about the team going out for bonding bevvy sessions. Do you think that's what teams in other countries do when they are in a slump? Go out on the skite? Can't you just see Gabriel Battistuta going into Fabio Capello's office and saying, 'Listen, boss, our form's a bit dodgy. What should we do?' And Capello rubs his chin before drawing on all his experience and says, 'I know. Go out and get pissed.' Can't see it. The idea that you can be a better team because you drink a lot, how does this rest with a Presbyterian club? We're sure in the past Messrs Gascoigne, McCoist, Hateley, Durrant and Co. liked and had many's a night out, but we bet you it wasn't anything like as often as the press or the players themselves made out. Excessive bevvying improves your football? Surely a Scottish footballing myth up there with 'Chick Young really does support St Mirren' and 'Stephane Bonnes really does exist'.

MONDAY, 5 MARCH

The stooshie over this new Celtic jersey just won't die down. In the midst of it all, though, you should spare a thought for the Celtic mascot. Does this mean he'll have to change his name to 'Hoopless the Huddle Hound'?

TUESDAY, 6 MARCH

If you have to stay in on a Saturday night then last Saturday night was a good one to have to stay in on, if you know what we mean. Real Madrid v. Barcelona. Not a bad pairing, up there with all the great glamour rivalries, like Inter Milan and AC Milan or Morton and St Mirren.

Of course, this isn't just a game of football, this is the chance for two players to stake their claims for the title 'Best in the World'. For Barca there's Rivaldo with emaciated, 'one of the undead' look, and for Real there was, of course, Figo, who looks like Mike Mercury, the Gerry Anderson puppet who used to drive Supercar – wee reference for the old folks there.

Of the two, Rivaldo definitely took the honours, with a stunning double and a third 'goal' that was controversially disallowed. What a player the Brazilian is. His eyes are sunk so deeply into his napper he can obviously see out the back of his head – his awareness is superb.

Incidentally, congratulations to commentator Rob Palmer. A full *five* minutes into his commentary before he mentioned England's victory against Spain. No disrespect to our game, but the standard in Spain, we would suggest, is just that wee bit better. They've got shooting down to a fine art and tackling down to a martial art. Boabby Carlos' lunge at Rivaldo and the way Kluivert's elbow connected with Hierro's chin; quality.

'CRAIG BROWN'

Errr, weelll, yeeesss, I suppose a lot of people want to know the answer to the big question that could seriously affect the future of Scottish football. But I might as well tell you right now, I will not disclose whether I chucked her or she chucked me, so there. To be quite honest, I'd much rather concentrate on which of the exciting new talents I will be picking for the next Scotland squad: Craig Dargo, Barry Nicholson, Charlie Miller or Gary MacAllister.

By the way, what about that shameful carry-on with Neil Lennon and a section of the Northern Ireland fans. That's one thing about Scotland fans – they don't care about religion or who a player plays for, they only boo players for being rotten regardless of religion or team.

Errrmmm, yes, I was interested in the Belgium/San Marino result. 10–1. Quite impressive. I'm a great admirer of the Belgians, especially their chocolate, and the team are no' bad either. They brought on a guy called Peeters. You know, I didn't recognise him without the dark specs and his partner, Lee.

The Foot and Mouth outbreak? Well, yes, it does affect Scotland. After all, we have a reputation for selecting auld coos.

Incidentally, I heard that last week some lucky punter with more money than sense bought a statue of a giant hamster at the Millennium Dome. I have to admit, I'd no idea they'd even heard of Tommy McLean down there.

WEDNESDAY, 7 MARCH

What was the biggest shock? Mel C announcing that she was quitting The Spice Girls or the fact that Rangers weren't linked with a move for her? OK, it's all turning pear-shaped at Castle Greyskull but is that any reason for all the daft stories linking everyone and their granny to the Teddy Bears?

At least Marcus Gayle was a real one. A former £4 million-rated striker snapped up for a bargain £900,000 without the gaffer ever having seen him. Bit of a lucky dip that, is it not? Apparently Marcus is another Christian – company for Saint Bert – although Gayle's church, to whom he'll be handing over a fair bit of the contents of his pay poke, has been described in some circles as 'a sinister cult'. What do you mean like the Masons?

Of all the guys linked with a move to Ibrox, two are worth closer examination. The Belgian bloke, Vermant, or something. He's a right dog and if nothing else he certainly *looks* like a Rangers player. The second worth mentioning is David Ginola. Just what a struggling Rangers side need. A lazy, diving, glamour boy. Or was this just a marketing ploy, a commercial department initiative? Stick Frenchman's coupon on shampoo bottle, stick Rangers badge on bottle, get bottle into superstore pronto, or bring out Ginola wigs for the fans to wear and have fun in, help them forget a wretched season?

SATURDAY, 10 MARCH

Big Dean Windass. We've always thought he looked a bit like a famous comic-book character. One who liked to eat cow pies and shaved with a blow-torch, in other words Desperate Dan. Well, have Middlesbrough not just – providing they get the paperwork sorted – snapped him up from Bradford. According to stories, Middlesbrough really wanted the striker Dani, but seems they have had to settle for Desperate Dani instead.

Sepp Blatter, who according to current rumours is a self-confessed big Celtic fan – they're all coming out the woodwork now, eh? – seems pretty adamant. Professional referees are coming. Fine. The SFA, however, are wondering where they're going to get the money to pay their whistlers. Well, how about sponsorship? We're sure Hugh Dallas could get fixed up with a double-glazing company, and John Rowbotham with a furniture polish business, while some of the others could be looking to tie up with a company with which they share a name: Kenny Clark, say, with Arnold Clark: Willie Young with Young's Seafood; and Mike McCurry with Curry's or, better still, The Ashoka.

THIS WEEK'S SPECIAL GUEST:

'TOMMY BURNS'

Errr, this is very, very true. It's looking good for Celticfootballclub but, errr, I won't be counting my chickens before the creme eggs have hatched. Against Hearts I didn't think we played all that well, but we still won and that is the mark of a team that isn't playing well but is still winning. I think. Even big Joos had an off day. It's not often Valgaeren plays more like Val Doonican, but there you go.

Still, we, errr, got the result and now face Dundee United in the semi-final. Dundee United did very, very, very well to beat Rangers. Great to see David Hannah getting the goal, the boy ran himself into the ground. His feet must have been very, very sore. In fact, I heard he had new boots on and his feet were killing him, but the good news for David is they're bringing out a video of his achievements called *Hannah and His Blisters*.

Hibs must fancy their chances of Cup glory. They haven't won the Cup for 99 years and must feel they are due a turn. Apparently they played really well that day back in nineteen-canteen – well, Gerry McNee says they did and he should know 'cos he was there.

But there's no point in looking back. We should always look forward or at least sideways, so I think it's very, very quite good that Kylie Minogue has got right behind a scheme to help Scottish footballers. At least, I think that's what they meant when they said Kylie was getting involved in a promotion aimed at supporting diddies.

ONLY AN EXCUSE?

TUESDAY, 13 MARCH

Sorry, but it's just one of those names that always makes us smile. Paddy Flannery. Maybe it's because his name was immortalised by Rhona Mcleod one day on *Sportsound*, when a slip of the tongue turned Paddy Flannery into Fanny Pladdery. For our money the funniest moment in the history of broadcasting. However, it wasn't for his name that Paddy was making the headlines recently. He's been in trouble with the law after a gesture made towards Cowdenbeath fans at the Stadium of Beath. According to reports, Flannery made a two-fingered gesture to the home support numbering some 100 fans. That's when we knew it was a stitch-up. One hundred Cowdenbeath fans? Who are they kidding.

Roy Essandoh's last-minute goal for Wycombe against Leicester. That's what the Cup is all about and that just about sums up football. There's a bloke playing in Finland answers an appeal on Teletext, gets a game, and scores a glorious and historic winner. And the bloke's a Motherwell reject as well. Anyway, we just wanted you to know that we too responded to that appeal, but Laurie Sanchez didn't take it seriously or, who knows, that could have been one of us achieving FA Cup immortality.

WEDNESDAY, 14 MARCH

There's an Old Firm tale, probably apocryphal, about Jock Wallace telling substitute Jim Denny to warm up. Denny got out the dug-out and made to head for the Celtic end. Wallace asked his player, 'Tell me, Jim, why are you going down that end?' – or something similar – to which Denny allegedly answered,

'They [the Celtic fans] give me a lot less stick then them [the Rangers fans].'

If the story isn't true then it should be. So what's your point, caller? The point is that 'Hell hath no fury like a Teddy Bear scorned'. They are an unforgiving lot, the Castle Grayskull faithful, so right now this current Rangers team probably feel more relaxed about playing in front of the fans of any team in Scotland except their own.

Take the Motherwell match. When Rangers went 1–0 down after only a few minutes at Fir Park most people were probably thinking that was the Sons of William gubbed again. But back they came, battling like Bears, scored an equaliser then nicked a winner right at the end. Sighs of relief all round, especially for David Murray. He must have been particularly delighted with the win because it meant he didn't need to fork out for a new player the next day. Isn't that what Rangers usually do after a defeat?

When the final whistle sounded Rangers players were hugging each other and punching the air as if they had done something remarkable – like won the Cup, or pulled Celtic's lead back to just 13 points, or escaped from having to face the wrath of Advocaat again.

Rangers won the match with a late, late goal from Robert 'Bob' Malcolm. Arguably, though, Malcolm – the current lumber of Miss Scotland – should not have been on the pitch following his interesting tackle on Said Chiba. If he could only trap a ball the way he did the Motherwell player's head. Word is that, although the referee and his assistant missed it, Mad Mental Malky could still face disciplinary action with video evidence being used to nail him.

Is this the way football is going? OK, most grounds have

CCTV, but are they now going to have them facing the pitch as well? If officials just did their jobs properly the video argument wouldn't be an issue because it wouldn't be necessary. How could a referee and a linesman miss this incident? Is it because it's Rangers? Don't be ridiculous, that's just unsubstantiated paranoia. Is it because it was Robert Malcolm and he's winching Miss Scotland and they want to keep in with him in case they get an introduction to some of her modelling pals? It all starts to make sense, doesn't it?

THURSDAY, 15 MARCH

It may be sheer coincidence – or something that we've just made up – but in Masonic circles Ibrox Stadium is known as the *Big Brother* house because all the talk is of who's leaving and who'll remain. But we have a sneaking suspicion that Dick Advocaat just might have a problem off-loading some of his duds. This must be doing the Little Captain's – he's been demoted from General – napper in.

He's in a bit of a *Catch 22* situation. Knowing he must qualify for the Champions League but also knowing that his squad – even with all his injured stars back – is just not up to it. Correction, make that just not up *for* it. There's no doubting the ability of many current Rangers players but do they have the heart for it? Has Advocaat lost the dressing-room, and if he has, where did he lose it and is there a reward for anyone who hands it into the nearest police station?

We noticed that Advocaat's name was linked to the vacant Spurs job, but stranger still that the names of Graeme Souness and George Graham had been linked with Ibrox. Personally we don't think either managers' style is what Rangers need at the moment. Souness is too much gung-ho while Graham is too much bung-ho. For the moment, though, the priority for Rangers remains the Champions League and it's starting to seem that no matter how bad they are, they are going to make it.

SUNDAY, 18 MARCH

One down, two to go? It's looking like it for Celtic. There are many people saying this will go down in history as the Larsson final, but we're not so sure. The Dallas final might be more appropriate. Is it just us or can Shuggie the D. sometimes, maybe, just be ever so slightly confrontational with certain players?

Who could we be talking about? Oh, we don't know. Off the top of our heads, say . . . Chris Sutton? Sending off a tad harsh maybe? Perhaps it wouldn't have been if Dallas had already booked the Celtic forward for persistent fouling in the first half. There must have been half a dozen occasions when Sutton ended up on his bum claiming he'd been fouled only for the free kick to be given the other way. Now, if on all of these occasions – as Dallas indicated – it was Sutton who was 'at it', then surely a yellow card should have been wheeched out long before the red was brandished with such relish.

And what about Freddie Dindeleux? Bobby Williamson was so embarrassed by Dallas' reluctance to send off the already booked Killie defender for consistently fouling Larsson that he removed Freddie from the field of play for him.

Hugh Dallas is an excellent referee but yesterday he was a model of inconsistency. Fastidiously forcing players to take free kicks from the exact spot maybe a yard from where they were preparing to take it from; one minute allowing late tackles the next minute coming down hard on them – even the fact that both teams were wearing their away strips was down to the official. Too much white otherwise. Maybe Hughie just wanted to re-establish himself after that Champions League shocker he had officiating in the AC Milan v. Deportivo match. Or maybe he was just hoping to be pelted by more cigarette lighters so he could get a wee business going in Argyle Street: 'Erra lighters now, three for a pound.'

So what about Larsson, then? The second goal was lucky, the first merely an overhead kick, but the third – well, it wasn't bad, was it? That wee shimmy – described by Archie MacPherson as a 'Highland Scottische' – that sold the dummy to Big Marsh was pure class. One debate, though, continues to rage. *We* can't make up our minds but what do you think? When did Larsson move quicker? When he was getting away from the Kilmarnock defence to score that third goal, or when he was getting away from Peter Martin's riveting post-match interview?

So, just what is the best league in Europe? Take the Champions League. Three teams from England, three from Spain, one from Turkey and one from, inevitably, Germany. Take the UEFA Cup Semi-Finals. Two from Spain, one from England, one from Germany. So, just what is now the best league in Europe?

Forgive us, we don't mean to be too controversial here, but we think it might *not* be ours. That we can live with. The fact that it might be the English league or, as they arrogantly call it, The Football League, on the other hand, just doesn't bear thinking about. As we see it, there is only one way to be spared the crowing of Messrs Hill, Davies, Motson, Atkinson, Venison et al. and that's for all those foreign Johnnies to make sure it's not an English team that lifts either of the European trophies.

So, let's be sensible about this. Why don't we threaten never to go to Spain for our holidays again if the Spanish clubs don't take care of Liverpool, Arsenal or Leeds. And as for Manchester United and Bayern Munich, maybe Alan McInally – who we think may have played for Bayern in Munich in Germany – could have *ein vee vord* with his former club and let them know what this would mean to us. No offence, Sir Fergie.

'CHICK YOUNG'

Ho! Ho! Ho! Yes, this is me, Chick Young, standing where I am, which is here. And let me tell you what a quite astonishing, totally sensational, miss-it-at-your-peril week I've had. Tom Hendrie has been promising us a big, high-profile, totally futile signing, and last week I thought we had it so that's why I was strutting along the corridors of the BBC singing.

> There's only one Jorge Cadet-ey,
> He puts the ball in the nett-y,
> He's Portuguese
> But thanks to Foot and Mouth Disease,
> He won't be coming to play for my beloved Saint Buddies!

Actually, to be totally and sensationally honest, this is one thing that's gone wrong that can't be blamed on Foot and Mouth Disease. Crazy Jorge won't be coming to St Mirren because they simply cannot match his wage demands. When I heard the news I phoned up Jorge and asked him if, within the sanity of his own nut, he was ready to come back to Scotland? He said he was. I then asked him if he was his own man now and he said, 'Hold on, I'll just ask my wife.' Shame, but there you go. I haven't given up, though. I still think Dundee United can be caught. In fact, I still think Rangers can be caught and St Mirren could still nick that Champions League slot!

Now, I have to say, anyone listening to *Sportsound* on Saturday will have heard Richard Gordon going on about me whipping off my designer gear and my mock leopard-skin Ys à la Billy Connolly and streaking across the pitch if St Mirren stay up. In fact, some people are saying I have already streaked on television, but this is not true. I can totally and sensationally categorically deny that the belly chasing the bloke in the Reebok advert is me.

SATURDAY, 24 MARCH

So, Mark Viduka is being linked with a move to Serie A with Lazio, said to be 'very keen' to get the big Aussie's signature. Viduka has stepped into the spotlight to clear up the situation. He says he's happy at Leeds and is going nowhere. So, there you have it, Mark has spoken. Expect him to join Lazio in the summer.

SUNDAY, 25 MARCH

What about Didier Agathe, then? Brilliant, eh? No, not the new deal he's been offered at Celtic Park, the burd. Did you see her picture in the papers? She looks like a cross between Gwyneth Palthrow and, well, Gwyneth Palthrow. In other words, she looks like Gwyneth Palthrow.

What is it about Old Firm players and their ability to pull such stunning women? I mean, no offence, we're not for one second suggesting that Didier isn't a handsome Dan, but we'd be interested to know if he was winching this young lady when he was with Hibs? We're just jealous? Of course.

Neither of us was at Hampden Park on Saturday. We were both otherwise engaged and we both found out the score just after five o'clock. On face value 2–2 seemed a good result. We started spouting platitudes to each other along the lines of, 'If, before the match, you'd offered Craig Brown a draw he would have grabbed it', and, 'Belgium are a class team, there's nothing wrong with a draw with a team of that quality'. Then we found out the story behind that 2–2 draw and, well, to be honest, it felt like a defeat, didn't it?

If there's a way to be gubbed 2–2 then surely Scotland's the only footballing nation in the world who could discover it. What a start to the match as well. Maybe that was the problem. Two goals up, them down to ten men, Billy Dodds on fire. If the fans were mystified about how well things were going, what must the players themselves have been thinking? Turning-point of the match, though, had to be Barry Ferguson's chance to make it three. If that had gone in then that would have finished it. Ach, who are we kidding? If that had gone in then that would mean it would have ended up a 3–3 draw. Got to hand it to Billy Dodds all the same. The way he nicked in front of Dozy Valgaeren to score that first goal. Wonder if Dick Advocaat was watching?

And our second goal? What about that Belgian bloke on the line? What a wimp! If that was a Scotsman in similar circumstances, he would have stuck his face in front of the ball rather than raise his hands. The guy deserved to go off, not for deliberate handball but for abject cowardice. And what about Billy Dodds' finish? Was that no' done with pure aplomb or what? No' bad for a guy that's hardly played all season.

OK, so we're 2–0 up and cruising, albeit in a cruiser with a spluttering engine. In the second half, though, the Belgians garnered all their talent, determination and sense of being hard-done-by and proceeded to run a humph on us. Like Rocky in *Rocky I, II, III, IV* and *V*, they just kept on coming. Pulled one back then, right at the death, hit us with a sucker punch. Bad enough that we lose a late, late equaliser, but we allow it to be scored by the guy with the worst hairstyle on the park.

What a difference 45 minutes make. From party atmosphere to a blamefest with Craig Brown the chief target. Questions abounded about the Scotland boss. Why didn't he use all his subs when Scotland were visibly tiring? Where did he get those chib marks on his napper? Anyway, it doesn't really matter now. It's all over bar the recriminations. If you want our view, it all started to go wrong the previous evening when it was decided to allow wives and girlfriends to visit the squad. Knees definitely seemed to weaken as the match went on. Anyway, what's that line about whatever will be will be? Bring on the San Marino!

'WALTER SMITH'

Well, obviously, particularly, at the present moment, I'm enjoying the break. It's great to get away from a football-mad city like Liverpool to the relative calm of Glasgow. I was up for John Brown's testimonial dinner and obviously, at the present moment, I have to say I didn't particularly enjoy the meal itself because, seeing as it was Bomber's 'do', they served the steak raw.

Obviously, it was particularly great to meet up with so many Rangers legends again and at the present moment, I see no one has yet bucked up the courage to tell John Greig his dentures are too big. But it was a great night. John Brown, I would have to say, is the last of a special breed, that special breed of ginger-haired Scottish footballers. We won't see many more like him, mainly because young red-haired kids today, first chance they get, dye their hair peroxide blond.

Obviously, I don't suppose it's been very easy for the Rangers support recently. In fact, I've heard their form has been so poor that, this year, many supporters' clubs are holding back their Player of the Year award – or just giving it to Hugh Dallas, which seems a good choice. He's definitely been Rangers' most consistent referee all season.

By the way, I will be coming back to Glasgow to visit Hampden Park later in the year. Sadly, Rangers didn't make the Cup Final so won't be playing there but, more importantly, Bon Jovi will be. Keep on, particularly, rocking.

TUESDAY, 27 MARCH

With this weekend's signing deadline rapidly approaching there must be a few clubs getting ready to make a couple of desperate buys as they try to make the top six or escape relegation. That being the case, might we suggest Oscar-winner Russell Crowe? Crowe, it seems, plays 'soccer'. He does. Apparently, during the filming of *Gladiator*, Crowe and his pals used to play five-a-sides but were asked to stop because the games were too physical and the producers were afraid their star might get hurt. What, Maximus pull a hamstring or damage a cruciate? No way. And just think, Motherwell have just lost Andy Goram. Who better to replace him than a mental case standing in goal wearing a skirt saying, 'I am goalie-ator'.

WEDNESDAY, 28 MARCH

We were just wondering. In the week when that great rapper, Puff Daddy, announced he was changing his name to 'P. Diddy', would Bert Konterman announce he was changing his name to 'A. Diddy'.

Did he have a shocker – again – or what? We think the guy needs a makeover. He needs to get running lessons and he needs to get something done about that hair of his. Mistakes always look even worse with that big curly fringe dangling in front of his coupon. A visit to Taylor Ferguson's is surely required.

In fairness to the Teddy Bears there were mitigating circumstances in this latest shambolic performance – too many of their top players were back. At least, this was the line D.A. seemed to be taking. So, what's the Little General going to do about it? Well, he's drawn up a list of some 20 players that he wants to sign. Given his record in the transfer market, that can't be allaying many fears. Does D.A. even intend to be here? Forget his on-field problems. Hairlase, the company that provide him with his locks, are pulling out of Scotland.

But possibly the only thing worse than being a Rangers fan at the moment is being a Hibs fan. Do the Hibees look like a team who believe they can finish second? Apparently, after the performance against St Johnstone, Alex McLeish took a long time to come out of the dressing-room and face the press. Wonder if he was trying to get Martin O'Neill on the phone to ask him if he was sure he didn't want Latapy?

See, when you think about it, Alex McLeish and Dick Advocaat, there are similarities. Alex chews lots of gum and Dick spends a lot of time having hairs planted in his head. So, with Alex it's Wrigleys while with Dick it's wigleys.

THURSDAY, 29 MARCH

We take it everyone at Spurs – indeed everyone involved in football in England – has forgotten the reason Glenn Hoddle was stripped of the England job? Glenn, it seems, is born again, again. Don't think much of his team all the same, and we wonder if he does either. We were just wondering if the first thing he did was tell the Tottenham players that the reason they were at White Hart Lane was for sins they committed in a previous life?

SATURDAY, 31 MARCH

Celebrity chef Gordon Ramsay is always referred to as 'ex-Rangers player'. How many games did he actually play for Rangers (Reserves), though? The same goes for Rod Stewart.

A trialist at Brentford, was it? How many games did he actually play?

Which brings us to our point. Is Stewart actually any good? His soccer abilities have reached mythological proportions, but any time we've ever turned up to see him play – between us, three occasions – he's been relatively anonymous right up until the point he went off injured after approximately half an hour. OK, it's up to him if he chooses not to wear shin pads inside his leopard-skin tights. Perhaps the reason Rod's football talents continue to garner publicity is because he's got his own football team. Does that sound like the actions of a decent player? Forming your own football team so that you can be the star player? Dosh can buy you everything but genuine fitba' cred. Sorry, but we reckon football is to Rod Stewart what karate was to Elvis Presley.

APRIL 2001

SUNDAY, 1 APRIL 2001

All week the transfer talk around Celtic Park was of Russell Latapy – didn't happen, lucky escape? – then on Saturday it was Caniggia who, according to certain sources, was set to move to Parkhead. The Celtic Board are said to be very keen that the Argentinian moves to Celtic. Because he's a class footballer? Don't be ridiculous. Because they reckon they could make a fortune selling Caniggia wigs?

TUESDAY, 3 APRIL

Whatever our affiliations we should all be grateful to Mark Viduka. Remember when he went down South? Remember the sneering about how easy it was to score in Scotland? Now the big man has banged in 20 goals, many English scribes are now grudgingly conceding that maybe he was scoring all those goals up in Jockland because he was actually quite good and not because our League is substandard.

WEDNESDAY, 4 APRIL

Neither of us have ever seen him play, but that Italian defender, Nandrolone, must be a right hard ticket when you look at the number of careers he's finished. Latest to fall foul of his attentions, Portuguese internationalist Fernando Couto. Some newspapers described the big defender as 'former Rangers target Couto'. As we remember it, his name and Rangers once appeared in the same paragraph, but that hardly made him a target, did it? All the same, Couto would have fitted in well at Ibrox. He was the only player we've ever seen with hair big enough to take the place of Dave MacPherson.

THURSDAY, 5 APRIL

Did you read about the Hearts players having stuff nicked from their lockers while they were training at Musselburgh Sports Centre. Apparently, one of the players had his £700 Gucci watch nicked. Admit it, what did you think when you read this: 'That's terrible', or, 'One of those diddies can afford a £700 watch'?

'STEWART MILNE'

Fit like, ken. As you'll have gathered from reading the newspapers or using your satellites to tune into Grampian television, I've been having a hell of a time of it at lately here at Aiberdeen. It's been like The Alamo up here. Things were so bad I thought I was going to have to start wearing my Davy Crockett hat again.

After last week's St Johnstone match, I was sitting in my luxury deckchair in my executive office just next to the pie shed at Pittodrie and one of the club officials popped his head round the door to say, 'That's anither twa drapped.' At first I wasn't sure what he was talking about – points, Board members, or if another of our young players had just reached puberty.

There's been a lot of bad blood in the boardroom recently but, you know, I have to say, personally speaking for myself, I canna stand big-heids. But until somebody as brilliant as me comes in, then who better to run this great piece of real estate ... er ... mean ... er ... this great club than the Stewarty boy. All in all, I'd have to say I think it's been a fantastically successful season for us – beyond our wildest dreams. Knocked out the Cup by a top-class team who made it all the way to the semi-finals, and OK, it's now starting to look like we might not make the 'top six'. But we don't look as if we're going to make the 'bottom' one either and that, for Aiberdeen, is a great season.

You ken this, though? Sometimes I feel folk in fitba' take things too far. I mean, I've just seen the news headlines: 'Milosevic Arrested'. A wee bitty drastic that, is it no'? OK, he didn't exactly set the heather on fire when he played for Aston Villa, but surely he wasnae *that* bad?

ONLY AN EXCUSE?

SUNDAY, 8 APRIL

As you would expect there were plenty of celebs at Celtic Park on Saturday: Billy Connolly, Jimmy Nail, Russell Crowe – whoops, sorry, it wasn't Russell Crowe, it was Jim White with his latest hairstyle. Maybe if Graham 'Greedy Ba's' Fenton had squared that ball to Stephen 'Totally Unmarked' McPhee instead of going for glory, then it might have been a totally different match but as it was, St Mirren passed up their best opportunity to cause an upset, and minutes later Tommy Johnson – who's touch evoked memories of Harald Bratbaak – netted what was always going to be the winner.

By the way, as a matter of interest, has anyone asked Tommy Johnson about his first touch prior to his goal? We might be doing the guy a great injustice. Maybe he meant it. A dummy that looks like a mistake, has that been done before? Who knows, you might be sitting watching the Spanish football next week and see Rivaldo try the exact same move.

And how's about this for a rarity? To all of you out there who don't believe in the Loch Ness Monster or the Yeti or Stephane Bonnes, wasn't that the latter we spotted on the pitch on Saturday?

Quite often, occasions such as these can be ruined by unwanted pitch invasions, but the human chain formed by the stewards did its job admirably. So much so that not even Matt McGlone got on.

A wee word about the Celtic Tenors. Was there some kind of showbiz deal in place whereby we weren't allowed to see them only hear them? It certainly added a touch of surreal farce to the whole occasion. When Mr Tenor hit that high note at the end of 'You'll Never Walk Alone', we bet every dog in Glasgow heard it, while we were deeply concerned for what it might be doing to the equipment on any aeroplanes flying overhead. And what about that operatic version of 'We Are the Champions'? Next time they should just hire that bloke who looks nothing like Freddie Mercury to do it.

Into the dressing-room and the champagne was flowing – 'Celtic Champagne', of course, which no doubt the Board sold to the team at cost price – while Chris Sutton's in-depth post-match analysis with Sky's David Tanner was interrupted by some of the Celtic lads pouring beer over Sutton's napper. And didn't Chris look pleased! The players then poured beer over Tanner's napper. And didn't David look . . . er . . . bemused! This was Celtic's day and not even the news of an imminent challenge to the legality of Catholic schools could dampen it.

Epilogue

Now, by this time on the last occasion Celtic won the Championship, their manager had resigned, casting the club into turmoil and putting something of a dampner on proceedings. Perhaps some Celtic fans, as they recovered from the mother, father, auntie and uncle of all hangovers on Monday morning may have remembered this. Then again, maybe they had trouble even remembering their own names.

So far nothing so catastrophic has happened this week, so after so many false dawns is this the real thing? Naturally, the press are already taking the 'Aye, OK, they've won the League but what are they going to do in Europe?' line. Scottish clubs can't generate the amount of dosh even diddy teams in England can secure due to current television deals, so they've got to rely on other things – like the ability to spot a bargain, the ability to motivate, tactical awareness etc. etc. etc. Well, Celtic might already have some of that. OK, there's no way they're going to win the Champions League, but if Celtic – or Rangers, for that matter – could emulate, say, Sturm Graz – a side, incidentally, put together for under £5 million – then that would be a good start, would it no'?

OK, money would be needed even to achieve Sturm Graz status in Europe, so how does Celtic raise this dosh? There have been rumblings which suggest Major Tim, Dermot Desmond (or is it Desmond Dermot?) is contemplating a shares issue. But what the Celtic support really want to hear from Desmond or Dermot is, when's he going to do something about that daft moustache of his?

But, hey, this is not the time for Celtic fans to be worrying about future European gubbings. It's time for absorbing the 'Tic vibes permeating the air. The era of the Hoops could be upon us. Don't believe us? Did you check out Sean Connery's kilt in America? The tartan was green. And what about yon Tiger Woods? Wins some pitch-and-putt competition and what does he get as his prize? A green blazer. How much more conclusive proof do you want?

MONDAY, 9 APRIL

The history of the Old Firm and the history of gloating are somehow intertwined. After all, what use is it if your half of the Old Firm gets one over on the other half and you can't have at least one full day of rubbing it into your workmates or getting pissed and singing party songs in the middle of the street at three o'clock in the morning?

The street parties at the weekend? Surely all the Irish flags and emblems were just to celebrate what Irishman Martin O'Neill has done for Celtic, just as last year's Oranje Day was all about what the Dutch contingent had done for Rangers. Right? Every year the ante is raised. If Celtic make it two in a row? Cardinal Winning becomes Pope Jinky I and declares Celtic Park a free state? And what if Rangers come roaring back under their new manager, George Graham? A summer of anti-Timic marches? No, wait, hold on, they do that anyway.

'KENNY DALGLISH'

Maybes aye, maybes naw, could be, could no' be, but I still think Celtic acted too hasty when they got rid of John Barnes. If only they'd held their nerve, then who knows what they might have achieved by now? As it is, they'll just have to settle for a possible treble. Well, that's up to them. I just want the Celtic supporters to know that, when Martin O'Neill legs it to Manchester United at the end of next season, me and John Barnes are standing by awaiting the call. We're ready to let bygones be bygones, come back to Celtic Park and start rebuilding the team around the spine of Dimitri Kharine, Oliver Tebily and Eyal Berkovic.

We've had a word with Graeme Souness and he says that, seeing as it's us, we can have Eyal back, he's just too hard working for the current Blackburn team. And we'd get the PR sorted out right from the start. We'd hire a right good company like that one run by the Countess of Wessex. She's a member of the Royal Family so you're guaranteed no cock-ups.

You know, it's funny to think that you've got to consider things like that when you're in football these days, but that's football for you. It's changing so much, almost as much as Anne Robinson's face when she moved to America. I mean, look at the drugs scandal at St Johnstone – although I hear that might be sorted out. George O'Boyle has been made an offer to join Raith Rovers and Kevin Thomas has been made an offer to join S Club 7.

SUNDAY, 15 APRIL

The site of all those sweetie papers and crisp pokes blowing around Hampden Park on Saturday served as a warning as to what a 'people's final' is really like. A day out for the whole family, sure, but that means a lot of picnics and screaming weans that get fed up after 20 minutes. No offence to Dundee United, but Celtic did us all a favour in reaching the Final. Now we'll have the Battle of the Greens, a Cup Final with an edge to it.

Hibs will be out to break their 500-year hoodoo and win their first Scottish Cup since 1501. Then there's Celtic. Of course, we know it's going to be a bit difficult for Rangers fans to support Hibs on Cup Final day, but once they consider what they'll have to go through should The Hoops actually complete the treble, then we're sure they'll manage.

MONDAY, 16 APRIL

So, the OVD Scottish Junior Cup Final will be a clash of the titans: Carnoustie v. Renfrew. Shame. No disrespect to Carnoustie or Renfrew, but we were so looking forward to some sort of Ayrshire involvement. OK, maybe an all-Ayrshire affair was too much to ask for, an impossible dream, but even one team from Burns Country would at least have provided an underlying threat of spontaneous mayhem. Now? Looks like we'll just have to content ourselves with honest endeavour and players with a superb third touch. Ho'd us back!

ONLY AN EXCUSE?

TUESDAY, 17 APRIL

Congratulations to Partick Thistle, newly crowned Champions of whatever league it is they are in. Last Saturday night the trendy West End of Glasgow must have been jumping with folk pretending to be Jags fans. Word is that for the next home game Thistle fans are going to dress up as pigeons as a tribute to what John Lambie has achieved for the club. Rumour has it that a bunch of media-types who frequent the Ubiquitous Chip were even considering erecting a symbolic doocot in their back court, but first they plan to have a pre-meet discussion, then a feasibility study so that they can establish just what a doocot actually is.

'SIR ALEX FERGUSON'

Oh yes, very proud. Very proud and very pleased to win the Premiership again, and very pleased with the performance of my players. I had no doubts about ex-Motherwell goalie Andy Goram. He did what was expected of him, came in and played like an ex-Motherwell goalie. I felt very sorry for Andy. Apparently a cleaner at the hotel he's staying at threw out a lot of his memorabilia. She thought the pile of newspaper clippings was rubbish and chucked them in the bin. The clippings were sitting on a pile of nude books and they went into the incinerator as well. The flute? He never mentioned that.

So, that's 14 major trophies in 14-and-a-half years at Old Trafford. Seven League Championships in nine years – this latest one making it three in a row. Of course, three in a row in England is like doing, say, 30 in a row in Scotland, but that's not to say I'm running down the Scottish game. Far from it. I keep in touch with what's happening North of the Border and let me tell you, it's a great place for young talented youngsters like Roy Ludovic and Jack Mathias to practise their trade.

But obviously, deep down, to be perfectly honest with you, I couldn't give a monkey's about Scottish football, I'm only really interested in Manchester United and my superb squad. I mean, on Saturday I could even afford to have David Beckham on the bench. Of course, I brought him on as a sub. I ask you, what other team in the world can take off a Butt and put on an arse?

ONLY AN EXCUSE?

WEDNESDAY, 18 APRIL

Neither of us have a tattoo, nor have we ever thought of having one done. So we can't really understand the motive behind Celtic fan Scott Wilson's decision to have a tribute to his hero scratched on to his entire back. No, hold on, maybe we can. If you were a Celtic supporter and your name was Scott Wilson then maybe you'd take drastic action too.

The tribute shows Henrik Larsson – arms outstretched and tongue outstretched – against the backdrop of a Swedish flag and reads 'King Henrik, The Magnificent 7'. And guess what? Surprise, surprise, every word is spelled correctly. Our thoughts flew back to that Rangers supporter a few years back who paid tribute to his hero by having 'McOist' written on his arm.

So the moral of the story? When having a tattoo done forget about safety, cleanliness and all that nonsense. Just make sure the bloke wi' the jaggy thing knows how to spell.

Scotland's American football team are, of course, the Claymores. How many of them are actually Scottish? We're not sure, but we think – possibly – one. So, why did the coaching staff show them *Braveheart* before their big opening match at Hampden Park? Who but a true Scot would be inspired by that film? We were just wondering how this affected the game itself? At the kick-off did the Scottish bloke shout 'Free-dom!!!' and get tore in while all his team-mates were busy baring their bums to the opposition?

FRIDAY, 20 APRIL

Deacon Blue are back, ya' beauty, ho'd us back. And guess who's
battering the skins for the Deeks? Yes, it's Dougie Vipond. No
doubt about it, rock n' roll's gain is *Sportscene*'s loss, if newspaper
reports are to be believed. Word is that Dougie's contract is up
for renewal and the BBC have told him he's an integral part
of the team. That's the television equivalent of the vote of
confidence from the chairman. OK, so Dougie – sorry about
this, I do apologise – isn't the smoothest or the coolest sports
presenter you've ever seen, but gie the bloke a chance and one
day he might be. And furthermore, we want to use him again
in *Only An Excuse?*.

SATURDAY, 21 APRIL

Did you happen to catch *Bad Boys International* on Channel Four
last week? A celebration of soccer bampotery *par excellence*.
Remember Cantona's kung-fu kick at that ned of a fan, then
how he completely blew his hard-man reputation with all that
rubbish about 'trawlers and seagulls and sardines'? He was
never the same after that. The show revelled in some South
American riots that were so good they put the Ayrshire Juniors
to shame. Tackling? Was that what they called it? Some of
the lunges, swipes and kicks delivered by the likes of Harris,
Hunter, Souness, Bremner and co. bordered on criminal assault.
And what about Harry Redknapp? How could such a growler
have had such a handsome son as Jamie?

Star of the show, though, was the Brazil nut, Edmundo.
Affectionately known as 'The Animal', this is surely the only
footballer in the world ever to have been convicted of plying

a monkey with drink. The occasion was his son's birthday and Ed decided it would be a great laugh to give the Chimp, hired as part of the entertainment, loads of swally. To be honest, in football circles we've never heard of a monkey being plied with drink, although we have heard of a few being spanked. Ultimately, though, we were left disappointed. A programme supposedly all about soccer psychos, and not so much as a mention of Gregor Stevens. Disgraceful.

Dick Advocaat is taking on Australia. Good, they need taken on. Any nation that gives the world *Neighbour*s and Rolf Harris deserves a square go with a pugnacious Dutchman. Hold on, though. The reason the Little General is taking on the Aussies has nothing to do with crap entertainers or soap operas. It's because Australia demanded that Craig Moore and Tony Vidmar be made available to play two worse-than-diddy teams in their World Cup-qualifying group. Quite right.

But wait, what's this? Louis van Gaal has asked Dick's advice on how to make sure Holland qualify for the World Cup Finals. And what, pray, was Advocaat's advice? Hammer the clubs who won't release players. Confused? Us as well.

And still with Hammers, here's a brammer. Big German Jorg has fairly been doing his bit to take the heat out of the next Old Firm match. According to Jorg, it's as we suspected. Rangers are rotten and that's the only reason Celtic won the League. But things will be different next season. By then Rangers will have signed some new players, there'll be no injuries and they'll win the title back. Dead simple. But who will these players be? Will Claudio Caniggia be one of them? We personally think so. Why? Because that's what the Teddy Bears have always done. Anyone plays a good game against them, Rangers sign them. Last year it was Kenny Miller and Allan Johnston – they had to wait for him. Before that it was Neil McCann, Billy Dodds and many, many more, all the way back to Colin MacAdam and Billy Urquhart. So, obviously, it's a policy that works well.

Such is the range of the all seeing eye of Sky Sports that at the weekend they could even show highlights of Yeovil v. Rushden and Diamonds. These days it seems that someone is covering every match being played in the entire country. If only that had been the case when Jim Baxter played. The highlights of the Scotland/England match are the only clips of Baxter in action that do any justice to his legend. All the other clips we've seen make 'Sixties football look ridiculously slow – a gentleman's game where everyone seems to be going out of their way to give each other lots of time and space.

We've enjoyed the radio tributes a wee bit better. Maybe because, with radio, you use your imagination that wee bit more. Bob Crampsey narrated a fine tribute on Radio Scotland. In it, it was rumoured that, at the time of Baxter's return to Ibrox, Jock Stein had made a move to sign him for Celtic. Maybe that would have been a better move for Baxter. Maybe Stein could have gotten more out of the Prodigal Son than Davie White. Of course, we'll never know. All we can do is try to imagine what it might have been like to have Jim Baxter and Jinky Johnstone at the same club. Forget about what might have happened on the pitch, can you imagine what they might have achieved off it? For a start, the St Enoch Hotel might still have been open to this day.

ONLY AN EXCUSE?

SUNDAY, 22 APRIL

The split? Right. A diddy idea from the word go. Apart from anything else, see this notion that you might end up playing a team three times away from home in a season. Crazy. To explain this away, the SPL have pointed out, 'Ah but, if you were disadvantaged this year, we'll redress that next year.' And if it happens that you don't make the top six next year?

Anyway, this plan of redress has given us an idea. There are 12 teams. If they all play each other four times that's 44 League games in a season. Too much, agreed. Play each other twice then. Twenty-two games. Too few. The solution? Play each other three times. Thirty-three games a season. Much better. Aye, OK, we know what that means, but surely by applying the same SPL logic – 'if you were disadvantaged this year we'll redress that next year' – that covers the anomalies of the League split. Bloody stupid idea? Correct. But any more stupid than what we've got now?

Did you happen to watch the presentation of the SPL trophy at Celtic Park? At first we thought a fan had taken a leaf out of Karl Power's book – the bloke who joined the Man U. team photo – and sneaked into the team line-up. He even got a hold of the trophy itself. But no, it wasn't some chancer, it was Stephane Bonnes. Please, Martin O'Neill, gonnae give this guy a game, or even just put him on as substitute for the last five minutes – something, anything, just once let us see Stephane Bonnes play and end all this confusion.

'CRAIG BROWN'

Errr, weeelll, how difficult is it for me to assemble a squad? Well, surely Scott Booth's recall says it all? In fairness to myself, Scott wasn't my first choice. I had another experienced striker in mind, but unfortunately I've no idea who Ted MacDougall's playing with these days.

But to be honest, I'd rather concentrate on some of the great young talent we've got in the squad for the Poland match. I'm thinking particularly of players like ... errr ... like ... errr ... I see that young Brazilian, the boy O, is back in training again. What a smashing young player Ronald O was before he injured himself trying some fancy-dan footwork. I bet you in future whenever he's in front of goal he'll settle for a good old-fashioned toe-winder instead of all that skill stuff.

Incidentally, I saw an interview with Bert Konterman on the television and the interviewer was talking about Rangers gubbing Dundee 3–0. He described it to Ronald as a 'handsome win'. Now there's a first, eh? Bert Konterman and the word 'handsome' in the same sentence.

But getting back to whatever it was I was talking about before I interrupted myself, what did you make of that rumour that Thomas Burns was being lured to Livingston by their chairman, Domincan Keane. I spoke to Thomas and he told me, 'As far as the stories go that I'm to join Livingstonmeadowbankferrantithistlefootballclub, this is very, very untrue.'

ONLY AN EXCUSE?

TUESDAY, 24 APRIL

We couldn't believe it. 'Give the boy a break!' we cried in unison when we heard Sir Trevor MacDonald announce that, coming up after the *News*, Fergie would be going on about fat. Sorry Trevor, we apologise. It was actually Sarah Ferguson talking about big bums and wobbly bellies and not, as we had wrongly assumed, Sir Alex getting tore into Charley Miller.

So, what about that wee diddy Poland match in Bydgoszcz? – which, incidentally, is pronounced 'Bydgoszcz' and comes from the old Polish word 'Byd-er-Gosszszszczzz', meaning 'Bydgoszcz'. See, you learn things in this column as well! An awful lot of friendly tackles flying about, were there not? Thankfully, the ref was right on the ball, and when Scott Booth tripped up Scott Booth inside the spot, the eagle-eyed official spotted it and awarded us the penalty kick that provided us with our thoroughly deserved victory.

But the really interesting thing to come out of this game against Poland was that we got to find out what happened to Celtic's old Poles, Darius Dowczek and Darius 'Jackie' Dziekanowski. Now there's a thing. See Darius out of Popstars, do you think he was named after either of these players? Dowczek, it seems, is now a highly successful manager in Poland while Dziekanowski has become a pundit. 'Jackie' said, 'I am like Charlie Nicholas, which is ironical and that speaks volumes for itself in spades.' Sorry, we have no idea whether Charlie had any contact with the former 'Polish George Best' when he was learning how to speak English.

WEDNESDAY, 25 APRIL

Perhaps even more impressive than his first touch, his pace, his stamina, his fitness, his overall ability and his hair condition given the amount of peroxide he's had on it, is Claudio Caniggia's ability to disappear quicker than a chief executive of Visit Scotland whenever straight questions need to be put to him? Come on, Claudio, ma man! What is happening with you and Los Teddos Bearos?

According to the press – no, not us, the *real* press – the deal was all but done. One magazine – *Hello* to be exact – even described the active Argie as 'Rangers new signing'. Now had that been *Hello, Hello* magazine, we might have believed it. Then, on top of all this, Caniggia's son, Alexander, appears in the newspapers wearing the hoops. Was this just Wee Sandy nailing his colours to the mast, or was this his old man's way of saying, 'Hey, Rangers, you-a better hurry up and-a dae something'?

Nicola Albani might be looking for an apology from Colin Hendry, but we have a wee suspicion that he won't be getting it. A six-month ban and a £4,000 fine? The best Nicola – isn't that a girl's name? – can expect is a rematch. After Braveheart gave the young San Marinoean, or San Marinesean, or whatever they call themselves, the Spanish Archer – el bow, get it? – what an outcry. Hendry was a disgrace. Hendry had besmirched the sporting name of Scotland. Hendry should be banished to obscurity – hold on, he's with Bolton Wanderers, he already is.

Now be honest, even although he was well out of order and was wrong and shouldn't have done it and deserves to be punished, it would be a shame if the career of someone like Hendry was to end this way. Forget the money. £4,000? Chickenfeed. Big Colin pays that as a retainer to the hairdresser who does his stylish mullet. It's the six-game ban that's the worry. Maybe after six games Hendry would still be fit and able to play for Scotland and could be recalled. Appeal? Definitely. Colin should be on the phone to FIFA right now asking them if they could maybe just double the number of games he's banned for. Well, better safe than sorry.

'GRAEME SOUNESS'

Can I just say something here? Yeah, for sure, there's something wrong with Rangers. They've turned into Celtic. Unfortunately, it's not the Celtic of today but the Celtic of a few years back. No disrespect to Celtic, but they were rubbish then. We always gubbed them and always the same way. (When I say 'we', of course, I mean my beloved Rangers team which Walter Smith did not do a bad job with.)

Anyway, the pattern in Old Firm games has been Celtic do all the early running, create all the chances, miss at least one sitter and then, in the second half, *bang!* We 'do' them. Now, ask yourself, what does that scenario remind you of? I'll give you a clue. Think Sunday, Rod Wallace, Ibrox Stadium. Yeah, for sure, I've never been one to criticise any one individual, so I'll just point the finger at the entire team. The main problem? There's no fight in this Rangers team. I tell you, when Graham Roberts was at Ibrox there was always plenty of fight. Mind you, that was mostly with me, but surely it's better a player fighting with his manager than no' fight at all . . . I think.

ONLY AN EXCUSE?

FRIDAY, 27 APRIL

If Andy Goram really did break Tommy Burns' heart then I'm sure Henrik Larsson has gone a long way towards putting it all back together again. Larsson, the newly crowned Scottish players' Player of the Year, is to Celtic what Laudrup and Gascoigne were to Rangers. Players who could be quiet, out of it, invisible even for almost an entire match then, just when the defence is thinking they have it sussed, flash of genius and it's all over.

Now, of course, there are Rangers fans who will say Larsson's not really *that* good, it's just that everyone else is rotten – which is exactly what Celtic fans used to say about Laudrup and Gascoigne. It happened when Laudrup and Gascoigne played in Scotland and it's happening to Larsson now. Rather than just enjoy watching good players, we become obsessed with questioning how good they really are just because they choose to be paid with Bank of Scotland notes. Even if grudgingly, surely it's time we show these guys some respect, because no matter what we think about them, no matter what we write about them, they're still better footballers than any pundit will ever be. And to that, I think Tommy Burns might say, 'This is very, very true.'

We read that Kenneth 'they think it's all over – it is now' Wolstenholme has been having a go at the number of women – 'soccer babes', as they are called – who are now involved in television football coverage. Gaby Yorath and Kirsty Gallacher immediately spring to mind. But surely they are there because they know so much about football and have so much to offer in terms of opinion and analysis? Anyway, we can't see what all the fuss is about, unless it's to do with the age of these soccer babes. Females in football are nothing new. The BBC have been using old women for years. Mark Lawrenson, Trevor Brooking, Jimmy Hill . . .

SATURDAY, 28 APRIL

What's going on at Manchester United? Keane blasts the team after they go out of Europe, now Becks blasts Keane. What's Fergie going to do to sort this out? Sit down and talk it through, or challenge David Beckham to a square go for having the cheek and audacity to challenge his beloved Woy? It would seem that success could rip this club apart.

We put it to you that Keane's swipe at the team could be interpreted in four ways. One, that as a concerned captain he was only speaking his mind – which he is, of course, entitled to do. Or two, he's trying to work his ticket out of the club – to Celtic, possibly . . . Or three, he's trying to provoke Davy Spice into leaving the club because he can't stand the idea of the young upstart earning more money than him . . . Or four, like his boss, he just likes a good fight? Brian Clough recently compared Roy Keane to Al Capone. We reckon that was a terrible thing to say – about Al Capone, that is.

MONDAY, 30 APRIL

Silence might be golden, but it certainly isn't Emerald Green. To those fans who couldn't resist breaking the proposed minute's silence for Jim Baxter at Ibrox on Sunday we ask, would it have been such an ordeal just to have held back for 60 seconds? (That's the number of seconds in a minute, just in case they were wondering.) Sixty wee, tiny, measly seconds of silence and then you can shout all you want for 90 minutes. Was that no' a good deal? If they knew they couldn't control themselves, then why not ask a pal to tie a gag on them, stick a scarf in their mouths, pull their ski caps down over their heads, anything but that shouting.

In the end the minute lasted approximately 30 seconds, and maybe that was something of a miracle in itself. Thank goodness we've left the bad old days of rampant sectarianism behind us. And thank goodness the players – many of whom enjoy the advantage of not having been brought up with the 'West of Scotland disease' all around them – have managed to rise up above the bigotry and the gloating to make the Old Firm matches nothing like as bad as they used to be.

Sarcasm? What, us? Just what is it with Old Firm players? If it's not taking a dump in a jacuzzi, it's hanging out windows winding up the fans below. According to reports we've read, one, possibly two Celtic players were guilty of stirring things up with the Rangers fans. How can you expect the fans to screw the bobbin when it comes to the 'get it right up you' factor when the players are almost – or, in some cases, are – just as bad as them? Banners and chants – good-natured abusive banter, for want of a better phrase – they're all fine. As long as it's just between the tens and thousands of fans, that's OK. Once the players start getting involved, then we could be getting into dangerous waters; then we really are talking the return of that great old Scottish football tradition, the 'Brekk-in'. What's going to happen next time Rangers hump Celtic? We shudder to think.

As for the match itself? Well, at the final whistle we reckon Dick Advocaat wished he could swap places with Dennis Tito, the world's first space tourist. Get out of Glasgow? The Little General must have wanted to get out of the universe as Rangers collapsed in front of their home crowd. Or did they collapse? Don't you need to be good in the first place before you can claim a collapse? The build-up to this game was along the lines that 'Rangers had a point to prove'. Well, we reckon that point was proved well and truly. No doubts about it now, no excuses, they are rotten. You really are left wondering what Advocaat has to do to revive this team.

The most telling part of Sunday's match, though, has to be the shots of Rangers fans streaming out of Ibrox before the final whistle. It's not the fact they were leaving that's interesting, it's the fact that Sky had gone to the trouble of setting up a camera to catch them walking down the street. How did they know that was going to happen? Have Rangers become just all too predictable?

MAY 2001

TUESDAY, 1 MAY 2001

Old Glasgow Empire story. Mike Winters is on stage doing his act and dying spectacularly. On wanders his brother, Bernie, pulling that big stupid face of his. From the audience they hear a voice groaning, 'J***s C****t, there's two of them!' Fast-forward to the present day, replace showbiz with football and the Glasgow Empire with Ibrox Stadium. Now, correct us if we're wrong but Dick Advocaat is still the Rangers' manager, isn't he? He hasn't been replaced by Ronald de Boer, has he? It's just that we seem to be reading a lot about Ronald having a word with his brother Frank about coming to Ibrox. Another de Boer? Another Dutchman? Another website? Just what Rangers need.

WEDNESDAY, 2 MAY

Football Stories on Channel Four. Last week it was all about the Charltons. Have to say, back in the 'Sixties we didn't realise just what a rebel Bobby was. His hair was much, much longer than George Best's, but only down the one side.

Apparently there are four Charlton brothers but one of them, Gordon, didn't appear at all in this programme. We wondered why. Maybe it's because he is the black sheep of the family, maybe he's bad for the family image, maybe he still has a full head of hair.

There can't have been many occasions when Celtic supporters wanted any team associated with Graeme Souness to do well. But this season a promotion for Blackburn Rovers would mean a permanent move to Ewood Park for Celtic's midfield workhorse,

ONLY AN EXCUSE?

Eyal Berkovic. Of course, a big question-mark hangs over the amount of money that will change hands. Between £3 million and £4 million has been mentioned, and with that kind of money we reckon a deal could definitely be done. Celtic, we reckon, would be more than willing to pay Blackburn between £3 million and £4 million to take Berkovic off their hands.

FRIDAY, 4 MAY

WEDNESDAY: Jan Wouters appointed Hard Man Coach at Ibrox.
FRIDAY: Exclusive interview on *Friday Night Sportscene*.

Three days? What took them so long? We thought they might have cancelled *Newsnight* on the Wednesday and had a half-hour special on Wouters and the brave new world that is Rangers, but no. Unbelievable. Word is Jan has been brought in to add a bit of steel to Rangers, a bit of grit, a bit of aggression – just what Barry Ferguson needs. But can you really turn a bunch of pampered under-achievers into SAS commandos overnight?

So, who is the man who answered the call when Dick Advocaat called out 'haunners'? We can exclusively give you ten things you probably already knew about Jan Wouters.
1. He is Dutch.
2. He played for Bayern Munich, which automatically makes him a good, good, great, great, personal friend of Alan McInally who, in case you might not be aware, once played for Bayern in Munich with Bayern in Germany.
3. He is from Holland.
4. He is a hard man.
5. He wasn't first choice. Rangers wanted Lee Marvin after the great job he did with *The Dirty Dozen*.

6. He doesn't attend the same Hairlase clinic as Dick Advocaat, but maybe he should.

7. He is from The Netherlands.

8. He once broke former Rangers idol Paul Gascoigne's jaw with his elbow.

9. He used to sport a dodgy 'tache just like the world's number one Rangers supporter, Graeme Souness.

10. He isn't Richard Gough.

SUNDAY 6 MAY

Beckham claims to be part-Jewish and that Judaism is the faith he is most familiar with. Beckham wears Eichmann tee-shirt at family birthday bash. Posh gives Becks earrings for birthday. Earrings are in shape of cross. Cross is Christian symbol. Beckham is mixed up or Beckham is just daft?

Why is it we just can't bear the idea of Leeds winning the Champions League. Is it because they're an English side and, as everyone knows, Scottish people just can't bear the idea of anyone English winning anything?

Don't be ridiculous. Their manager, David O'Leary, is, after all, Irish. Leeds United are the team forever associated with the greatest, red-headed, Scottish nyaff of all time, Billy Bremner. They've also got two great Scottish internationalists of yesteryear, Eddie Gray and Roy Aitken, in the dugout.

So, why can't we come to terms with the idea that Leeds could well become Champions of Europe? We have a perfectly sensible answer: Alan Smith. Sorry, but we just can't cope with the notion that a team which contains a face that we would never tire of slapping could go on to become champions of Europe. And if

ONLY AN EXCUSE?

that isn't a sound footballing reason for wanting Leeds to bomb in the Champions League, then we don't know what is.

So, Ronnie Biggs is back home in England. He's looking old and he's looking feeble so I suppose it's to be expected that there's already speculation linking him with Arsenal.

MONDAY, 7 MAY

Maybe he does bring a lot of it upon himself because of the slight hint of headmaster-like arrogance he displays on the pitch, but no referee takes more pelters, criticism and general dog's abuse than Motherwell's own Hugh Dallas. Interesting, though, that when Real Madrid's Roberto Carlos had a pop at Shug recently then suddenly the Dallas boy was our top whistler and the nation jumped to his defence. Basically, Boabby Carlos inferred that our League is a diddy league and no ref from such a diddy league should be in charge of a match as important as a Champions League semi-final. Now, Boabby had no right saying that. Of course, he's right. We do have a diddy league, but he has no right saying that. It's the unwritten law, only Scottish punters are allowed to slag off Scottish football and only Roger Mitchell is allowed to defend it.

'DAVY PROVAN'

Hello reader, yes reader, well reader, what a week it's been for Henrik Larsson. I just hope he can get over the shock of me not voting him my Man of the Match on Sunday. And staying with Celtic, I take my hat off to Andy Walker and his quality insinuation on Saturday's *Super Scoreboard* that the press 'made up' the story about the Celtic player's dressing-room celebrations at Ibrox. But I cannot agree with him. I mean, why on earth would the press in this country want to make up a story to discredit Celtic?

And still with the quality radio show that is *Super Scoreboard*, what about Billy Davies? 'Something is happening at Fir Park,' announced Nicky Docherty grimly and he was right, that something was nothing. Billy Davies wasn't there because he was in his kip with the dry boke. Not quite the same as having parted company with his club.

But if I can, for reasons of nothing more than I couldn't give a toss about Motherwell, move on to the subject of Hampden Park. Can I just say I'm absolutely convinced that the Cup Final will take care of itself but I'm seriously concerned about attendances for what will follow it. So, I really think the people of Scotland have got to get right behind the lads, so I would urge them all to go out now and buy their tickets for Bon Jovi.

Finally, can I just pass my best wishes on to Pedro Ricksen, the brother of Fernando Ricksen, who has been on trial with Partick Thistle. If Pedzo is anything like his brother, then let's hope a deal can be done. The First Division could always do with a few loony characters and I'm sure that he and John Lambie could strike up a relationship to rival Alf Ramsay and Bobby Moore, Jock Stein and Billy McNeill or even Bud Abbott and Lou Costello.

ONLY AN EXCUSE?

TUESDAY, 8 MAY

Did anyone happen to catch the women's FA Cup Final between Arsenal and Fulham on Monday afternoon? To be honest, it wasn't as bad as we thought it would be.

OK, so the best-looking bird on the pitch was the big chicken mascot at the toss-up, and when the cameras went into the dressing-room your first instinct was to shout, 'Get 'em on!', but the match itself was kind of exciting right up until the moment that all 22 players tired at the same time – about ten minutes into the second half. We have to say, though, we were concerned about the women spitting – so unladylike – and using words like 'bollocks' – which we were able to lip-read. We also feel that Fulham shot themselves in the foot by fielding a goalie under five feet in height. If only someone could invent high-heeled football boots.

WEDNESDAY, 9 MAY

When we heard that Bert Konterman – the David Icke of Ibrox – was blaming the Nandrolone situation on a bunch of Dutch coos, we immediately thought, that's a hell of a way to talk about your team-mates. But no, we got it wrong. The Dutch coos Bert was talking about weren't Ricksen, Numan, de Boer and co. but the coos back home in Holland. OK, given the way they've played this year, the idea of anyone on the playing staff at Ibrox being on any sort of performance-enhancing drug does seem ridiculous. However, the gospel according to Bert states that greedy farmers back in The Netherlands are pumping their cattle full of Nandrolone, and when players eat a burger or have a plate of mince and tatties at their maw's on a Sunday, they become infected.

OK, so we've all felt at some point that Nando Ricksen had to be on something, but cows on Nandrolone? Mind you, there's a thought. Have you ever been greyhound racing in Holland? Maybe they don't use hares, maybe they use cows: 'The cow's running at Greiyhoondersprinterstadt.' Nah, somehow doesn't sound feasible.

THURSDAY, 10 MAY

It takes a big man to do a big job, so for the big job at Ibrox they sent for a big man, Wee Tommy McLean. The Little, Little General has been saddled with the position of Director of Finding Great Young Players for Rangers and Making Sure They Pick Up Plenty of Injuries in Training.

He's been charged with the task of finding a Barry Ferguson – without the mental streak – every two years. This mission could, however, give Tommy a few problems. After all, does he know who Barry Ferguson is? Wee Tam kept referring to Y-Bazza as *Derek* Ferguson when fulfilling his role as Archie McWoaafffson's TV side-kick during last season's Champions League campaign. Of course, following the appointment of Jan Wouters, there wasn't even the slightest hint of 'we better get a Scotsman, preferably an ex-Ranger, to fill this post'.

Wee Tam's charges up at Tannadice were obviously pleased to see him go judging by the message they left on the windscreen of his car. You probably saw the words 'F*** Gers', but did you know that the word 'Thank' preceded them but melted quicker than the others?

We're sure, in time, Tommy will develop plenty of fresh, young, home-grown talented youngsters who will end up signing for Hearts and Kilmarnock while Rangers continue to sign ageing foreigners. And talking of Claudio Caniggia . . . bad move or just a terrible one? What do you think? Do you really believe he's committed to playing? Do you really believe he's worth the money? Do you really believe he's only 34? It's one thing turning on the odd flash of undoubted skill for Dundee, but Rangers fans tend to be that wee bit more demanding. If Caniggia doesn't equal Larsson's tally next season, the Teddies may label him a failure.

But then Claudio might just be one of the wee signings. There may be *mega* big ones on the way. Rangers are always being linked with Robbie Fowler, and then it was Robbie Savage so it surely follows that they should now be linked with Robbie Williams. Williams turned out for Port Vale last week in a testimonial. We're sure if Rangers came in with an offer he would jump at it. That would be a good move all the same. Rangers could then drop 'Simply the Best' and replace it with 'Let Me Entertain You', and instead of baring his bum for the Vale, Robbie could bare his bum for the 'Gers. We're sure the Ibrox faithful would appreciate his *craic* (crack).

FRIDAY, 11 MAY

Here's a question for you. Whatever happened to Ted McMinn? That's right, Rangers' Ted McMinn, the legendary 'Tin Man'? Where are they now? We'll tell you where. He's number two to Mark Wright, the new manager of Oxford United.

Obviously, Ted is there to pass on some of his special and unique skills – like how to be tripped on the halfway line and manage to fall in the box.

No offence but wasn't it great to see Leeds United go out of the

Champions League? It's not that we couldn't have coped with the notion of a Premiership club in the final, it's just that the prospect of Alan Smith picking up a medal was giving us the dry boke.

But what about the second semi? According to the commentary team, the mighty Real Madrid were knocked out by Owen Hargreaves. Of course, you realise that if Bayern Munich now go on and win it, then Hargreaves' presence in the team makes it as good as an English victory. We just can't win, can we?

'FERGUS McCANN'

When I heard they had found chewed electric cables inside Celtic Park I immediately thought, is gum not good enough any more, now they chew cables? Then I heard it was rats that were chewing the cables. Rats? I thought, smell the coffee! Have the old board tunnelled back in again. Turns out they're talking rodents. Can you believe it? Who'd have thought Martin O'Neill kept a 'durty hoose'.

You know, I look back at my time as El Presidente of Celtic Park with great fondness. Oh what fun it was dealing on a day-to-day basis with egocentric under-achievers, mediocre moaners and greedy rascals manipulating the media and the fans for their own ends – and Paulo di Canio, Jorge Cadete and Pierre van Hooijdonk weren't much better. Incidentally, did I tell you I was thinking of buying West Ham United? Not to make money, just so that I could fight with Paulo again.

Oh, just before I go, I've been asked to say a few words so I will and what's more I won't charge any fee. Now, I don't often give talks without having what I want to say written down on a piece of paper and stuck inside my hat, but here goes.

In this day and age of people who aren't really interested in football and who are only interested in making a lot of money, it's an honour to pay tribute to Tom Boyd.

Who is he again?

SATURDAY, 12 MAY

It is a great FA Cup tradition all the same, the singing of 'Abide with Me'. Bit of a waste of time putting the words up on the big screens, though. Your average Liverpool fan can't read. That was a nice touch getting the two fitba' opra babes to lead the singing. Only disappointment, though, came at the end of the number when they didn't swap jerseys.

But what about the Millennium Stadium? Impressed or what? As for the match itself? Duff or what? Apart, of course, from the last 15 minutes. Just when we were discussing whether you pronounce it Loongberg or Joongberg, wee Freddy turns out to be more of an Iceberg as he scores to put the Gunners one up. Even then you still had this feeling that Arsenal would rue all those chances they missed, and this turned out to be true.

Michael Owen: for someone with such an odd-shaped, out-sized head, the boy can fairly shift, and he knows how to find the onion bag. We don't know if you noticed, but did you see Prince Andrew having a wee word with Owen when the His Lowness was being introduced to the players before the kick-off? Wonder if Andy was saying, 'One has a ten spot on you bagging a double'? Neither of us are what you would call royal watchers, but we were both disappointed when they cut away from Prince Andy just at the crucial bit of the national anthem. We still don't know whether he sings 'God save the Queen' or 'God save my Mum'.

ONLY AN EXCUSE?

SUNDAY, 13 MAY

Kilmarnock fans must be delighted. OK, their team still haven't claimed the coveted knocked-out-in-the-first-round-of-the-UEFA-Cup slot, but hey, never mind, Super Ally did get another chance to say cheerio for now to the Rangers fans.

We felt for Bobby Williamson. Didn't anyone tell the interviewers on radio and television that Bobby is actually the manager of Kilmarnock and not Ally McCoist's agent? It was actually starting to get embarrassing, the fawning that went on. Anyway, it was nice of Dick Advocaat – that's right, the *Rangers* boss – to send out Ally – the *Kilmarnock* player – for another final cheer. Funny that, we had no idea Dick was boss of Killie as well.

MONDAY, 14 MAY

Dario Bonetti's no mug. He obviously knows his history. It's a well-known fact that if you applaud the champions on to the pitch then you invariably end up gubbing them. And lo, that's what happened to Celtic on Sunday. Dundee, who have always been entertaining every time we've seen them this season, deserved the victory, and Celtic didn't hit the magical 100 points; they've still only got 97. How many teams in Scotland would settle for that sort of disappointment?

What is it about footballers these days? They can't see green cheese. One has an 'exotic dancer' for a girlfriend, they've all got to have one. First it was Didier Agathe, now it's Tommy Lovenkrands. Used to be Tennants Lovelies, the obligatory models, the occasional Miss Scotland, even the odd Page-Three

Stunna was your average footballer's chick/wife. But they all seem a bit tame now. So, we detect a trend here. We predict that, within a year, a lap dancer will be *the* 'must-have' accessory for your young Scottish footballer. All we can say is, we do have sympathy for those footballers whose wives have embarrassing occupations like nurses or school-teachers.

WEDNESDAY, 16 MAY

Yes, it was entertaining, but the greatest European final of all time? Come on. Do teams not have to play well to qualify for that honour? The only reason we got a goalfest in the UEFA Cup Final was because Liverpool and Alaves defended like pub teams. OK, we'll hold our hands up and admit that, when it comes to the fitba', we always – for some inexplicable reason – find it difficult to get behind the English team, but on this occasion we were glad that Liverpool won because it spared the nation the sight and sound of millions of Liverpudlians whingeing on about how they 'never get nuttin'.

We enjoyed the shots of Gerard Houllier on the bench all the same. Some managers go ballistic, some stand motionless. Houllier? He talks to himself. And we're not talking the odd sweary mutter, we're talking a full two-way conversation between Gerard and Gerard. Watch him the next time Liverpool make a Cup final, hopefully in about another 20 years time.

They say all great games need tension. Given that goals were being scored so freely then surely this match was, therefore, bereft of tension. Not so. Throughout the entire game we were kept wondering: Barry Davies, will he/won't he just come right out and profess his love for Michael Owen? And by the way, didn't you feel sorry for Jordi Cruyff. If you've ever played a match – any match – with your old man watching, you'll know how bad it is. Can you imagine what it must be like playing with your old man watching you and your old man is Johan Cruyff? Cannae be easy. I mean, it's not as if Jordi can turn to his faither and say, 'OK, then, could you have done any better?'

FRIDAY, 18 MAY

We really enjoyed that promotional video for Rangers' new training complex – or, to give it it's other name, the *Friday Night Sportscene* exclusive. We're surprised Rangers bother with a PR department when they've got the BBC. To be honest, there wasn't really much to see which means, no doubt, we'll have to sit through another exclusive tour of Auchenhowie once it's finished.

Wee Dick did seem pretty proud of the medical department, though. Forget Wee Tam McLean, if things continue as they have been, then whoever's running that place is going to be an extremely busy man. We're sure it'll look great and it's bound to be slightly better than piling into a minibus and driving to some park somewhere, but will it really change things dramatically? After all, did the 'Gers have an academy when they were winning their nine in a row and doing really well in Europe? Is Auchenhowie truly vital for the future, or is it just one huge, big, red, white and blue herring?

'DENIS LAW'

Well, you know, as I say, I couldn't believe it when I heard that Sir Alex Ferguson was going to cut all his Manchester United ties. That's a very drastic step to take, cutting all your ties, because you might have to go to something formal and you've got to wear a suit and, of course, a tie, and you go to your wardrobe and all your ties are cut up. Mind you, it was only his Manchester United ties he cut. He might have some other ties that he bought out of maybe Marks and Spencers or Next or What Everys. Anyway, listen, Alex, if you need a loan of a tie – or a suit even – give me a shout. I've still got the stuff I nicked off Joe Baker when I legged it from Turino.

But, hey, listen, I'm being serious here because the big question now is, will Sir Alex of Fergie be at Manchester United for the start of next season, or will he do the honourable thing and walk out the door with his head held high and join Manchester City like what I did?

But, you know, as I say, the only thing you can predict about football is its unpredictability, so who would have thought that the SFA would want Kenny Dalglish to be named Scotland's Roaming in the Gloaming Ambassador for their Euro 2008 bid. They see him as being like our version of their version of Michel Platini, or something like that. Well, no offence to Kenny, but how will the Europeans – especially those from Europe – understand a word that he says? He mumbles and people can't understand him. They really should have gone for someone who speaks clearly ... and people can't understand him. Someone like, say, off the top of my head, *me*. Anyway, 2008 Euros? How much is that in pounds?

ONLY AN EXCUSE?

SATURDAY, 19 MAY

The Scottish Junior Cup Final. What a pity about the name of the sponsors, OVD. It sounds like something you hope the doctor will never say to you.

Shame that the name is so open to cheap, smutty jokes like that last one given this Cup Final is such a family occasion. By 'family occasion' we mean, of course, that the stadium – in this case, Firhill – is full of middle-aged women wearing newly knitted scarves and bewildered looks on their faces, and loads of bored weans playing 'tig'.

Hats off to Archie MacPherson and Billy Stark who managed to stay awake and keep talking throughout the entire 90 minutes, plus four minutes' injury time, plus 30 minutes' extra time, plus the penalty shoot-out. And hats off to STV for putting aside the fact that they probably didn't want to be there and occasionally remembering to fire in some jazzy graphics, thus giving the whole event that 'real' football feel.

Carnoustie Panmure – now there's a name that says 'football legends' – had their chances: approximately one – no, make that two barrowloads full, but failed to take any. By the time we reached the penalty shoot-out, you couldn't help but think that the jinx of the team who wears the Arsenal-style tops was about to strike again.

Now, of course, it must be hellish for the poor blokes taking them, but you have to admit penalty shoot-outs are much more exciting than the 'golden goal'. Mind you, so tired did most of the players look in extra time that a golden pass to the intended target would have been an achievement, never mind a golden goal. Underdogs – and dogs is the right word: some of the close-ups of the players; pure growlers – Renfrew missed two penalties, handing the initiative to Carnoustie. But the favourites were a flash in the Panmures as they blew both chances. The Renfrew goalie, who had deservedly been named Man of the Match, then saved a penalty and, when his team-mate stroked the next one home, Renfrew were victorious. What we're not sure, though, is what winning the OVD Scottish Junior Cup ultimately means? Gaining you entry into Europe or just guaranteeing you a couple of boxes of rum to drink on the bus home?

MONDAY, 21 MAY

They think it's all over? It is now. Ally McCoist has finally hung up his lead boots. The end of an era. If we have one complaint it's that not enough media coverage has been given to this event. But Ally's no' daft, is he? OK, so he didn't score in his farewell game, but when *Shot at Glory* finally comes out then, in the public's perception, the Cup Final between Kilnockie and Rangers will be Ally's last game. And what does he do in that – one, two or is it three goals in the Cup Final? Then Rangers will sign him to team up with Caniggia and it all begins again.

All together now (to the tune of 'Mud, Mud, Glorious Mud'): 'Hearts, Hearts, moaning faced Hearts . . .'. Right, that's enough. We're sure everyone in the West of Scotland feels ever so sorry that Edinburgh's Jam Tarts didn't make Europe. The fact that Craig Levein has already said that – had he been in a similar situation – he would have done exactly the same as Martin O'Neill, has largely been ignored by Hearts supporters generally and some of his players in particular. Cheated? So, it was all down to that one game, was it? Come on, Jambos, don't kid yourself. Kilmarnock did you a favour by beating Celtic. Now it's them who have to worry about drawing a decent team in the UEFA Cup and having their season start with a Euro-tanking.

However, all this anti-Celtic rhetoric – not like Hearts – is, we feel, just a diversionary tactic, a smokescreen to obscure the number of former Jambo favourites slinking out the side door – guys like, wait for it, Stevey Fulton. The man they called Baggio has been told to get on his Bikio by The Great Leveinski. But questions have to be asked. What is really at the root of Fulton receiving the rubber ear? Is it to save some money on wages, or is it to save vast amounts of money on the players' catering bill?

TUESDAY, 22 MAY

At the moment things are going well for Celtic – apart from them losing their last three games. While they're queuing up to get out of Ibrox, there seems to be a line-up outside Martin O'Neill's door of players desperate to sign on the dotted line and extend their contracts. Two trophies in the bag, the third to be played for on Saturday, the balance has shifted so dramatically don't be surprised if Sean Connery starts coming back to Celtic Park.

And yet, despite all this, a black cloud hangs over Parkhead that won't go away: the link between Martin O'Neill and Manchester United. The rumour factory has been working overtime on this one. It is a classic Scottish football rumour in that the more the man in question denies it, the more the rumours persist. In fact, so persistent are the rumours in the face of denial that you might be forgiven for thinking some footie journos in the press and elsewhere were maybe just publishing their dreams and wishes rather than hard facts. What are we getting at? Are we saying that there are a lot of Manchester

United fans among the sporting media up here in Scotland who would just love to see Martin join United? Exactly. Nothing to do with a campaign to put the wind up the Tims who are just getting a wee bit too cocky? Of course not. As if that sort of thing goes on in Scotland.

WEDNESDAY, 23 MAY

Surprise, surprise, the Champion's League final was decided on penalties but there, dare we say it, the similarities with the Scottish Junior Cup final end. The lack of goalmouth action in the San Siro was down to two extremely talented teams cancelling each other out rather than at Firhill a few days earlier where the lack of goalmouth action was down to two extremely knackered teams.

We did feel a bit sorry for Valencia's peroxide protector of the onion bag, Canizares, right at the end although we're not quite sure why he was crying. Was it because he lost, was it because he just realised how ridiculous he looked with his stockings pulled up over his knees or was it because he's seen himself on telly and realised he needed his roots done? Incidentally, did you happen to notice the number of grubby hand marks on the trophy itself? You'd have thought with all the money spent and all the attention to detail and all the planning to make the Champion's League final a special occasion that someone might have remembered to bring a tin of Brasso.

ONLY AN EXCUSE?

THURSDAY, 24 MAY

Tattoos, body piercing, flash cars, big house, expensive holidays, designer gear, all of that we can understand but David Beckham's latest fashion statement has got us beat. Who would have thought that walking around with a fanny on your head would ever become fashionable. Can we also just take this opportunity to be really pedantic and point out that Beckham's hairstyle should not be called 'a Mohican' because it isn't 'a Mohican'. As any student of the book or even the movie 'Last of the Mohicans' will tell you, the Mohicans in the film, Uncas and his old man Chingachcook, had long flowing locks. The guys with the mental shaved hairstyles like the one sported by Beckham were the Hurons whose leader aff was called? Quick? Have to hurry you? That's right, Magua. So, next time your down the boozer and you hear someone call Beckham's new barnet 'a Mohican' you can stand up and with great confidence tell them they are wrong. PS If you happen to get a sore face for your troubles, we accept no responsibility whatsoever.

FRIDAY, 25 MAY

We're still mulling over the unexpected exit of Jorg Albertz from Rangers, surely the act which more than any other would seem to hint that there just might be something not quite right within the once impregnable ramparts of Castle Greyskull. Phrases like 'forced out', 'no choice but to leave' and 'act of betrayal' are being bandied about and yet 'The Hammer' has also been saying he had no problems with Dick Advocaat, no problem with the other players, loved the fans and wasn't leaving Scotland because his burd had chucked him. So, the REAL reason Jorg has Hamburgered off back to Germany?

Well, all we can think of is that Germans have a reputation for having no sense of humour and at the moment there's just too much laughter inside Ibrox.

Incidentally, just in case you were wondering, we're afraid the answer is 'no', I'm afraid we have no idea why Jorg Albertz was given the Bank of Scotland Player of the Month Award either.

SATURDAY, 26 MAY

It was the Rangers' fans last chance for the season, Hibs to prevent Celtic from doing the unthinkable. Well, it didn't happen. With ruthless efficiency The Hoops routed the Hibs and completed their much sought after treble. Fair enough, Hibernian did play quite well but when you think about it, Celtic scored three goals, Colgan made two great stops and one decent one and Rab Douglas didn't have a thing to do – apart, of course, from coming for a couple of crosses and giving the Celtic fans a few heart attacks. That, we suppose, says it all does it no'? But what about the Cup Final as an event? Does it match up to other national cup finals like say, off the top of our heads, the English one? Well, at least we actually have the Scottish Cup final taking place in Scotland unlike the English who have to go to Wales. Unlike the FA Cup Final we have no communal singing of 'Abide With Me' nor do we have the National Anthem. Given the two sides involved today would a wee blast of the Wolfetones playing 'The Soldiers Song' been unreasonable to expect? We don't know how the viewing figures broke down but we have the feeling that most people who started with the BBC stuck with it. Once they'd got over the shock of Dougie Donnelly not wearing a tie they, no doubt, become enthralled in the war of words between Darren Jackson and Willie Miller.

ONLY AN EXCUSE?

By war of words we don't mean they were arguing, we mean they seemed to be having a competition to see who could come up with the most grammatical errors. Sky started in epic style with stirring music from the movie 'Gladiator'. We kind of half expected to cut to Russell Crowe in the studio saying, 'My name is Commentator'. At the end of the day, though, Celtic were worthy winners and for them it was time to celebrate. As for the Hibees? Well, every cloud has a silver lining so at least being losers the Hibs players didn't have to suffer any of David Tanner's legendary after-match interviews.

SUNDAY, 27 MAY

Forget the Cup Final, the big result over the weekend was, of course, a Rangers Old Crocks Select – or 'Heroes' as they called themselves – beating Linfield 6–2 in the final of The Heroes Cup. We're not saying it was a fix or anything but if the team is called the Rangers Heroes and the trophy is called the Heroes Challenge Cup then who do you think is supposed to win it?

Looking at a photograph of the Rangers line-up we had to say that hardly any of their faces had changed and I bet they are all grateful for that – apart from, maybe, Davy Dodds.

MONDAY, 28 MAY

The season is over. Summer spreads out before us like a vast, never-ending, empty desert. How will we survive without our football? Our lives will be empty. There will be nothing happening. Nothing to read about, to argue about, to pontificate about. At times it can become so unbearable we even find ourselves wishing that the newspapers would just make something up but, we all know, there's just no way they would ever do anything like that. So, all we can do is wonder what will have happened and what will be happening when that glorious day dawns and another season begins in but a few long, long, long weeks time.

Will Alex McLeish have any hair left after accepting the West Ham job and having daily meetings with Paulo di Canio? Will debt-ridden Morton, Airdrie and Clydebank survive or will they merge to form a super-debt ridden club called Mordriebank or Clytonair? Will anyone have seen Ally McCoist's movie? Will the potatoes have come up nice on Hampden Park? What will the average age of the Motherwell team be next season, 14? Will Jim McLean finally get his shot at Mike Tyson? Will Maradona finally make his debut for Dundee? Will St. Johnstone season ticket sales finally reach double figures? If Livingston do well, will Jim Leishman start up with those rotten poems of his again? If Livingston do badly will Jim Leishman start up with those rotten poems of his again? Will Sir Alex Ferguson buy Aberdeen and turn this club from a sleeping giant into a snoozing giant? Can St. Mirren come straight back up so that they can go straight back down again? Can Kilmarnock's domination of that hotbed of Scottish football, Ayrshire, continue? Will Ian Ferguson get booed the next time he plays for Dunfermline against Celtic? Will Martin O'Neill find Champion's League glory . . . with Manchester United? How many more Dutchmen will there be at Rangers and will the name Auchenhowie have been changed to Aaachenhouije? Only time – and Bob Crampsey's 'Now You Know' – will tell.